slow cooker
100 everyday recipes

First published in 2011
LOVE FOOD is an imprint of Parragon Books Ltd

Parragon
Chartist House
15-17 Trim Street
Bath BA1 1HA, UK
www.parragon.com

ISBN: 978-1-4454-4716-2

Printed in China

Produced by Ivy Contract
Cover and additional internal photography by Mike Cooper
Cover and additional home economy and food styling by Lincoln Jefferson
New recipes written by Christine France

Notes for the Reader

This book uses imperial, metric, and US cup measurements. Follow the same units of measurement throughout; do not mix imperial and metric. All spoon measurements are level: teaspoons are assumed to be 5 ml, and tablespoons are assumed to be 15 ml. Unless otherwise stated, milk is assumed to be whole, eggs and individual vegetables, such as potatoes, are medium, and pepper is freshly ground black pepper.

The times given are an approximate guide only. Preparation times differ according to the techniques used by different people and the cooking times may also vary from those given as a result of the type of oven used. Optional ingredients, variations, or serving suggestions have not been included in the calculations.

Recipes using raw or very lightly cooked eggs should be avoided by infants, the elderly, pregnant women, convalescents, and anyone with a chronic condition. Pregnant and breast-feeding women are advised to avoid eating peanuts and peanut products. People with nut allergies should be aware that some of the prepared ingredients used in the recipes in this book may contain nuts. Always check the package before use.

Vegetarians should be aware that some of the ready-made ingredients used in the recipes in this book may contain animal products. Always check the packaging before use.

slow cooker

introduction

For busy people, a slow cooker can provide that most elusive culinary combination: healthy home-cooked food *and* convenience. With minimum effort, you can serve up a meal that is tender and flavorsome while saving time and money—what could be better? Just put the ingredients into the slow cooker in the morning, switch it on and leave it to cook while you go to work and get on with your life. As the slow cooker cooks at a very low temperature, cooking times are quite flexible—you needn't worry about your meal burning if you are late home.

For the health conscious, slow cooking doesn't require much oil, and the nutrients in vegetables stay in the pot rather than being lost through boiling and draining. Slow cooking makes cheaper, tougher cuts of meat deliciously tender, saving you money on your shopping and, because a slow cooker only uses as much electricity as a lightbulb, it will cut down your electric bill too! All kinds of dishes can be prepared, and because everything is cooked in one pot there is less washing-up to do afterwards.

This book will introduce you to the range of sumptuous meals that you can prepare in your slow cooker, from warming winter casseroles, low-fat vegetable soups, and spicy curries to indulgent desserts. There are dishes to suit every occasion and taste with a mouthwatering selection of meals that are suitable for all the family. All it needs is some planning and preparation in advance so you can be assured that the perfect meal will be waiting for you when you return at the end of the day.

All the recipes featured in this book will fit into an 8-pint capacity slow cooker. Models vary slightly from one manufacturer to another, so make sure you check the instructions for your particular slow cooker, however the basics apply to all models. So turn the page, choose a recipe for a simple starter or a magnificent main course, and get ready to save money, eat healthily, and rediscover time just for you.

to start

chicken noodle soup

ingredients

serves 4

1 onion, diced
2 celery stalks, diced
2 carrots, diced
2 lb 4 oz/1 kg chicken
3 cups hot chicken stock
4 oz/115 g dried egg tagliatelle
2 tbsp chopped fresh dill,
    plus extra for serving
salt and pepper

method

1 Preheat the slow cooker, if necessary, or according
to the manufacturer's directions.

2 Place the onion, celery, and carrots in the slow cooker.
Season the chicken all over with salt and pepper and
place on top. Pour the stock over. Cover and cook on
low for 5 hours.

3 Carefully lift out the chicken and remove the meat
from the carcass, discarding the bones and skin.
Cut the meat into bite-size pieces.

4 Skim the excess fat from the juices, then return the
chicken to the slow cooker. Turn the setting to high.

5 Bring a large saucepan of lightly salted water to a boil.
Add the tagliatelle, return to a boil, and cook for
5 minutes. Drain well.

6 Stir the tagliatelle and dill into the pot, cover, and
cook on high for an additional 20 minutes. Serve
immediately, in large bowls, sprinkled with dill.

clam chowder

ingredients

serves 4

2 tbsp butter
1 onion, finely chopped
2 potatoes, peeled
    and cut into cubes
1 large carrot, diced
1¾ cups fish stock or water
10 oz/280 g canned clams,
    drained
1 cup heavy cream
salt and pepper
chopped fresh parsley, to garnish
fresh crusty bread, to serve

method

1 Preheat the slow cooker, if necessary, or according
   to the manufacturer's directions.

2 Melt the butter in a skillet, add the onion, and sauté
   over medium heat for 4–5 minutes, stirring, until the
   onion is golden.

3 Transfer the onion to the slow cooker with the
   potatoes, carrot, stock, and salt and pepper. Cover and
   cook on high for 3 hours.

4 Add the clams and the cream to the slow cooker and
   stir to mix evenly. Cover and cook for an additional
   1 hour.

5 Adjust the seasoning to taste, then sprinkle with
   parsley and serve with crusty bread.

carrot & cilantro soup

ingredients

serves 6

1 tbsp butter
1½ tbsp sunflower oil
1 Bermuda onion, finely chopped
3½ cups diced carrots
½-inch/1-cm piece fresh ginger,
    finely chopped
2 tsp ground coriander
1 tsp all-purpose flour
5 cups vegetable stock
⅔ cup sour cream
2 tbsp chopped fresh cilantro
salt and pepper
croutons, to serve

method

1 Preheat the slow cooker, if necessary, or according to the manufacturer's directions.

2 Melt the butter with the oil in a pan. Add the onion, carrots, and ginger, cover, and cook over low heat, stirring occasionally, for 8 minutes, until softened and just beginning to color.

3 Sprinkle over the ground coriander and flour and cook, stirring constantly, for 1 minute. Gradually stir in the stock, a little at a time, and bring to a boil, stirring constantly. Season to taste with salt and pepper.

4 Transfer the mixture to the slow cooker, cover, and cook on low for 4–5 hours. Ladle the soup into a food processor or blender, in batches if necessary, and process until smooth. Return the soup to the slow cooker and stir in the sour cream. Cover and cook the soup on low for an additional 15–20 minutes, until heated through.

5 Ladle the soup into warmed soup bowls, sprinkle with the cilantro, and top with croutons. Serve immediately.

tomato & lentil soup

ingredients

serves 4

2 tbsp sunflower oil
1 onion, chopped
1 garlic clove, finely chopped
2 celery stalks, chopped
2 carrots, chopped
1 tsp ground cumin
1 tsp ground coriander
¼ cup red or yellow lentils
1 tbsp tomato paste
5 cups vegetable stock
14 oz/400 g canned chopped
    tomatoes
1 bay leaf
salt and pepper
sour cream and toasted crusty
    bread, to serve

method

1 Preheat the slow cooker, if necessary, or according
   to the manufacturer's directions.

2 Heat the oil in a pan. Add the onion and garlic and
   cook over low heat, stirring occasionally, for 5 minutes,
   until softened. Stir in the celery and carrots and cook,
   stirring occasionally, for an additional 4 minutes. Stir
   in the cumin and coriander and cook, stirring, for
   1 minute, then add the lentils.

3 Mix the tomato paste with a little of the stock in a small
   bowl and add to the pan with the remaining stock, the
   tomatoes, and bay leaf. Bring to a boil, then transfer to
   the slow cooker. Stir well, cover, and cook on low for
   3½–4 hours.

4 Remove and discard the bay leaf. Transfer the soup
   to a food processor or blender and process until
   smooth. Season to taste with salt and pepper. Ladle
   into warmed soup bowls, top each with a swirl of
   sour cream, and serve immediately with toasted
   crusty bread.

greek bean & vegetable soup

ingredients

serves 4–6

2¼ cups dried navy beans,
　　soaked in cold water overnight
2 onions, finely chopped
2 garlic cloves, finely chopped
2 potatoes, chopped
2 carrots, chopped
2 tomatoes, peeled and chopped
2 celery stalks, chopped
4 tbsp extra virgin olive oil
1 bay leaf
salt and pepper
12 black olives and 2 tbsp chopped
　　fresh chives, to serve

method

1 Preheat the slow cooker, if necessary, or according
to the manufacturer's directions.

2 Drain the beans and rinse well under cold running
water. Place them in the slow cooker and add the
onions, garlic, potatoes, carrots, tomatoes, celery, olive
oil, and bay leaf.

3 Pour in 3 pints boiling water, making sure that all the
ingredients are fully submerged. Cover and cook on
low for 12 hours until the beans are tender.

4 Remove and discard the bay leaf. Season the soup to
taste with salt and pepper, and stir in the olives and
chives. Ladle into warmed soup bowls and serve.

chicken & leek soup

ingredients

serves 6-8

12 dried prunes, pitted, or
    12 plumped, dried prunes
4 chicken portions
4 cups sliced leeks
6¼ cups boiling chicken
    or beef stock
1 bouquet garni
salt and pepper

method

1 Preheat the slow cooker, if necessary, or according
to the manufacturer's directions.

2 If using dried prunes, place them in a bowl and add
cold water to cover. Let soak while the soup is cooking.

3 Place the chicken portions and leeks in the slow
cooker. Pour in the stock and add the bouquet garni.
Cover and cook on low for 7 hours.

4 If you are going to serve the chicken in the soup,
remove it from the cooker with a slotted spoon and
cut the meat off the bones. Cut it into bite-size pieces
and return it to the cooker. Otherwise, leave the
chicken portions in the slow cooker.

5 Drain the prunes, if necessary. Add the prunes to
the soup and season to taste with salt and pepper.
Re-cover and cook on high for 30 minutes.

6 Remove and discard the bouquet garni. Either ladle
the soup, including the cut-up chicken, into warmed
bowls or remove the chicken portions and keep warm
for the main course, then ladle the broth into warmed
bowls. Serve immediately.

bacon & lentil soup

ingredients

serves 6

1 lb/450 g thick, rindless smoked
    bacon strips, diced
1 onion, chopped
2 carrots, sliced
2 celery stalks, chopped
1 turnip, chopped
1 large potato, chopped
1/3 cup green lentils
1 bouquet garni
4 cups chicken stock or water
salt and pepper

method

1 Preheat the slow cooker, if necessary, or according
to the manufacturer's directions.

2 Heat a large, heavy pan. Add the bacon and cook over
low heat, stirring frequently, for 4–5 minutes, until the
fat runs. Add the onion, carrots, celery, turnip, and
potato and cook, stirring frequently, for 5 minutes.

3 Add the lentils and bouquet garni and pour in the
stock. Bring to a boil, then transfer the mixture to the
slow cooker. Cover and cook on low for 8–9 hours,
or until the lentils are tender.

4 Remove and discard the bouquet garni and season
the soup to taste with pepper and salt, if necessary.
Ladle into warmed soup bowls and serve.

spicy bean dip

ingredients

serves 6

2 tbsp corn oil
1 onion, finely chopped
2 garlic cloves, finely chopped
2–3 fresh green chiles,
    seeded and finely chopped
14 oz/400 g canned refried beans
    or red kidney beans
2 tbsp chili sauce or taco sauce
6 tbsp hot vegetable stock
1 cup grated cheddar cheese
salt and pepper
1 fresh red chile, seeded and
    shredded, to garnish
tortilla chips, to serve

method

1 Preheat the slow cooker, if necessary, or according to the manufacturer's directions.

2 Heat the oil in a large, heavy skillet. Add the onion, garlic, and chiles and cook, stirring occasionally, over low heat for 5 minutes until the onion is soft and translucent. Transfer the mixture to the slow cooker.

3 Add the refried beans to the slow cooker. If using red kidney beans, drain well and rinse under cold running water. Reserve 2 tablespoons of the beans and mash the remainder coarsely with a potato masher. Add all the beans to the slow cooker.

4 Add the sauce, hot stock, and grated cheese, season with salt and pepper, and stir well. Cover and cook on low for 2 hours.

5 Transfer the dip to a serving bowl, garnish with shredded red chile, and serve warm with tortilla chips on the side.

sweet & sour chicken wings

ingredients

serves 4–6

2 lb 4 oz/1 kg chicken wings,
    tips removed
2 celery stalks, chopped
3 cups hot chicken stock
2 tbsp cornstarch
3 tbsp white wine vinegar
    or rice vinegar
3 tbsp dark soy sauce
5 tbsp sweet chili sauce
¼ cup brown sugar
14 oz/400 g canned pineapple
    chunks in juice, drained
7 oz/200 g canned sliced bamboo
    shoots, drained and rinsed
½ yellow bell pepper, seeded
    and thinly sliced
½ red bell pepper, seeded
    and thinly sliced
salt

method

1 Preheat the slow cooker, if necessary, or according
    to the manufacturer's directions.

2 Put the chicken wings and celery in the slow cooker
    and season with salt. Pour in the chicken stock, cover,
    and cook on low for 5 hours.

3 Drain the chicken wings, reserving 1½ cups of the
    stock, and keep warm. Pour the reserved stock into
    a pan and stir in the cornstarch. Add the vinegar, soy
    sauce, and chili sauce. Place over a medium heat and
    stir in the sugar. Cook, stirring constantly, for 5 minutes,
    or until the sugar has dissolved completely and the
    sauce is thickened and smooth.

4 Lower the heat, stir in the pineapple, bamboo shoots,
    and bell peppers and simmer gently for 2–3 minutes.
    Stir in the chicken wings until they are thoroughly
    coated, then transfer to a serving platter.

warm garbanzo bean salad

ingredients

serves 6

1 cup dried garbanzo beans,
    soaked overnight in cold
    water and drained
1 cup pitted black olives
4 scallions, finely chopped
fresh parsley sprigs, to garnish
crusty bread, to serve

dressing

2 tbsp red wine vinegar
2 tbsp mixed chopped fresh herbs,
    such as parsley, rosemary,
    and thyme
3 garlic cloves, very finely chopped
1/2 cup extra virgin olive oil
salt and pepper

method

1 Preheat the slow cooker, if necessary, or according
   to the manufacturer's directions.

2 Place the garbanzo beans in the slow cooker and add
   sufficient boiling water to cover. Cover and cook on
   low for 12 hours.

3 Drain well and transfer to a bowl. Stir in the olives and
   chopped scallions.

4 To make the dressing, whisk together the vinegar,
   herbs, and garlic in a pitcher, and season with salt and
   pepper to taste. Gradually whisk in the olive oil. Pour
   the dressing over the still-warm garbanzos and toss
   lightly to coat. Garnish with the parsley sprigs and
   serve warm with crusty bread.

spicy baked beans

ingredients

serves 4–6

2½ cups dried white haricot beans,
    soaked overnight in cold water
    and drained
4 oz/115 g salt pork, soaked in cold
    water for 3 hours and drained
3 tbsp molasses
3 tbsp dark brown sugar
2 tsp dry mustard
1 onion, chopped
salt and pepper

method

1 Preheat the slow cooker, if necessary, or according
    to the manufacturer's directions.

2 Place the beans in the slow cooker and add about
    6¼ cups boiling water so that they are covered. Cover
    and cook on high for 3 hours. Meanwhile, cut the salt
    pork into chunks.

3 Drain the beans, reserving 1 cup of the cooking liquid.
    Mix the reserved liquid with the molasses, sugar,
    mustard, and 1 teaspoon of salt.

4 Return the beans to the slow cooker and add the salt
    pork, onion, and the molasses mixture. Stir, then cover,
    and cook on low for 11 hours. Adjust the seasoning,
    if necessary, and serve immediately.

spicy zucchini

ingredients

serves 6

2 lb 4 oz/1 kg zucchini, thickly
    sliced
1 onion, finely chopped
2 garlic cloves, finely chopped
2 red bell peppers, seeded and
    chopped
5 tbsp hot vegetable stock
4 tomatoes, peeled and chopped
2 tbsp butter, diced
salt and cayenne pepper

method

1 Preheat the slow cooker, if necessary, or according
   to the manufacturer's directions.

2 Place the zucchini, onion, garlic, and bell peppers in the
   slow cooker and season to taste with salt and cayenne
   pepper. Pour in the stock and mix well.

3 Sprinkle the chopped tomatoes on top and dot with
   the butter. Cover and cook on high for 2½ hours
   until tender.

eggplant cakes

ingredients

serves 4

3 tbsp olive oil, plus extra
    for greasing
2 onions, finely chopped
2 eggplants, halved with flesh
    removed and shells reserved
2 red bell peppers, seeded and
    chopped
1 large tomato, peeled and
    chopped
6 tbsp milk
2 egg yolks
pinch of ground cinnamon
1 cup finely grated fresh
    breadcrumbs
salt and pepper
fresh cilantro sprigs, to garnish

sauce

1¼ cups sour cream
3–4 tbsp sun-dried tomato paste
    (optional)

method

1 Preheat the slow cooker, if necessary, or according
  to the manufacturer's directions.

2 Heat the oil in a large, heavy skillet. Add the onions
  and cook over low heat for 5 minutes. Add the diced
  eggplant flesh, bell peppers, and tomato and cook for
  15–20 minutes until all the vegetables are soft. Transfer
  the mixture to a food processor or blender and process
  to a puree, then scrape into a bowl. Beat together the
  milk, egg yolks, cinnamon, and salt and pepper in a
  pitcher, then stir into the vegetable puree.

3 Brush 4 individual baking dishes or cups with oil and
  sprinkle with the breadcrumbs to coat. Mix some of
  the remaining crumbs into the vegetable puree. Slice
  the eggplant shells into strips and use them to line
  the dishes. Spoon the filling into the dishes, and fold
  the overlapping ends over the top.

4 Cover with foil and place in the slow cooker. Pour in
  sufficient boiling water to come about on third up the
  side of the dishes. Cover and cook on high for 2 hours.

5 To make the sauce, lightly beat the sour cream and
  add the tomato paste to taste, if using. Season with
  salt and pepper. Lift the dishes out of the cooker and
  remove the foil. Invert onto serving plates and serve
  with the sauce, garnished with cilantro sprigs.

stuffed cabbage with tomato sauce

ingredients

serves 6

1 cup mixed nuts, finely ground
2 onions, finely chopped
2 garlic cloves, finely chopped
2 celery stalks, finely chopped
1 cup grated cheddar cheese
1 tsp finely chopped thyme
2 eggs
1 tsp yeast extract
12 large green cabbage leaves

tomato sauce

2 tbsp sunflower oil
2 onions, chopped
2 garlic cloves, finely chopped
1 lb 5 oz/600 g canned
    chopped tomatoes
2 tbsp tomato paste
1½ tsp sugar
salt and pepper

method

1 Preheat the slow cooker, if necessary, or according to the manufacturer's directions.

2 First make the tomato sauce. Heat the oil in a heavy pan. Add the onions and cook over medium heat, stirring occasionally, for 5 minutes until softened. Stir in the garlic and cook for 1 minute, then add the tomatoes, tomato paste, sugar, and bay leaf. Season with salt and pepper and bring to a boil. Lower the heat and simmer gently for 20 minutes until thickened.

3 Meanwhile, mix the nuts, onions, garlic, celery, cheese, and thyme in a bowl. Lightly beat the eggs with the yeast extract in a pitcher, then stir into the nut mixture.

4 Cut out the thick stalk from the cabbage leaves. Blanch the leaves in a large pan of boiling water for 5 minutes, then drain, and refresh under cold water. Pat dry with paper towels. Place a little of the nut mixture on the stalk end of each cabbage leaf. Fold the sides over, then roll up to make a neat package.

5 Arrange the packages in the slow cooker, seam side down. Pour the sauce over the cabbage packages. Cover and cook on low for 3–4 hours. Serve the cabbage packages hot or cold.

everyday

chicken parmigiana

ingredients

serves 4

1 egg, beaten

4 skinless, boneless chicken breasts

heaping ¾ cup fine dry breadcrumbs

2 tbsp olive oil

12 oz/350 g prepared tomato-based pasta sauce

4 thin slices cheddar cheese

1 cup finely grated Parmesan cheese

salt and pepper

cooked rice, to serve

method

1 Preheat the slow cooker, if necessary, or according to the manufacturer's directions.

2 Season the egg with salt and pepper. Dip each chicken breast in the egg, turning to coat evenly, then dip into the breadcrumbs, lightly pressing down to cover evenly.

3 Heat the oil in a skillet over high heat, add the chicken breasts, and sauté quickly for 3–4 minutes, until golden brown, turning once.

4 Pour the pasta sauce into the slow cooker and place the chicken breasts on top. Cover and cook on low for 4 hours.

5 Place a slice of cheddar cheese on top of each chicken breast and sprinkle with Parmesan cheese. Cover and cook on high for an additional 20 minutes. Serve immediately with rice.

chicken & dumplings

ingredients

serves 4

2 tbsp olive oil
1 large onion, thinly sliced
2 carrots, cut into ¾-inch/
2-cm chunks
2 cups of 1-inch/2.5-cm green
bean pieces
4 skinless, boneless chicken breasts
1¼ cups chicken stock
salt and pepper

dumplings

1⅔ cups self-rising flour
½ cup lard
4 tbsp chopped fresh parsley

method

1 Preheat the slow cooker, if necessary, or according to the manufacturer's directions.

2 Heat 1 tablespoon of oil in a skillet, add the onion, and sauté over high heat for 3–4 minutes, or until golden. Place in the slow cooker with the carrots and beans.

3 Add the remaining oil to the skillet, then add the chicken breasts and sauté until golden, turning once. Arrange on top of the vegetables in a single layer, season well with salt and pepper, and pour over the stock. Cover and cook on low for 4 hours.

4 Turn the slow cooker up to high while making the dumplings. Sift the flour into a bowl, and rub in the lard. Stir in the parsley, and season to taste with salt and pepper. Stir in just enough cold water to make a firm dough, mixing lightly. Divide into 12 and shape into small balls.

5 Arrange the dumplings on top of the chicken, cover, and cook for 30 minutes on high. Serve immediately.

chicken & corn pot

ingredients

serves 4

3 tbsp corn oil
1 large onion, thinly sliced
1 green bell pepper,
    seeded and chopped
8 chicken pieces, such as thighs
    and drumsticks
14 oz/400 g canned chopped
    tomatoes, drained
pinch of cayenne pepper
1 tbsp Worcestershire sauce
1¼ cups boiling chicken stock
1 tbsp cornstarch
generous 1 cup frozen corn,
    thawed
generous 3 cups frozen
    fava beans, thawed
salt
crusty bread, to serve

method

1 Preheat the slow cooker, if necessary, or according to the manufacturer's directions.

2 Heat the oil in a large, heavy skillet. Add the onion and green bell pepper and cook over medium heat, stirring occasionally, for 5 minutes until the onion is softened. Using a slotted spoon, transfer the mixture to the slow cooker.

3 Add the chicken to the skillet and cook, turning occasionally, for 5 minutes until golden all over. Transfer to the slow cooker and add the tomatoes. Season with cayenne pepper and salt. Stir the Worcestershire sauce into the hot stock and pour into the slow cooker. Cover and cook on low for 6½ hours.

4 Mix the cornstarch to a paste with 2–3 tablespoons water and stir into the stew. Add the corn and beans, re-cover, and cook on high for 30–40 minutes until everything is cooked through and piping hot. Transfer the stew to warmed plates and serve with crusty bread.

chicken braised with red cabbage

ingredients

serves 4

2 tbsp sunflower oil
4 skinless chicken thighs
    or drumsticks
1 onion, chopped
5½ cups shredded red cabbage
2 apples, peeled and chopped
12 canned or cooked chestnuts,
    halved (optional)
½ tsp juniper berries
½ cup red wine
salt and pepper
fresh flat-leaf parsley,
    to garnish

method

1 Preheat the slow cooker, if necessary, or according to the manufacturer's directions.

2 Heat the oil in a large, heavy pan. Add the chicken and cook, turning frequently, for 5 minutes until golden on all sides. Using a slotted spoon transfer to a plate lined with paper towels.

3 Add the onion to the pan and cook over medium heat, stirring occasionally, until softened. Stir in the cabbage and the apples and cook, stirring occasionally, for 5 minutes. Add the chestnuts, if using, juniper berries, and wine and season to taste with salt and pepper. Bring to a boil.

4 Spoon half the cabbage mixture into the slow cooker, add the chicken pieces, then top with the remaining cabbage mixture. Cover and cook on low for 5 hours until the chicken is tender and cooked through. Serve immediately, garnished with the parsley.

slow cooked chicken & apples

ingredients

serves 4

1 tbsp olive oil

4 chicken portions, about
6 oz/175 g each

1 onion, chopped

2 celery stalks, coarsely chopped

1½ tbsp all-purpose flour

1¼ cups clear apple juice

⅔ cup chicken stock

1 cooking apple, cored
and cut into quarters

2 bay leaves

1–2 tsp honey

1 yellow bell pepper, seeded
and cut into chunks

salt and pepper

garnish

1 large or 2 medium eating apples,
cored and sliced

1 tbsp butter, melted

2 tbsp raw brown sugar

1 tbsp chopped fresh mint

method

1 Preheat the slow cooker, if necessary, or according
to the manufacturer's directions.

2 Heat the oil in a heavy skillet. Add the chicken and
cook over medium–high heat, turning frequently, for
10 minutes, until golden brown all over. Using a slotted
spoon, transfer the chicken to the slow cooker.

3 Add the onion and celery to the skillet and cook over
low heat, stirring occasionally, for 5 minutes, until
softened. Sprinkle in the flour and cook, stirring
constantly, for 2 minutes, then remove the skillet from
the heat. Gradually stir in the apple juice and stock,
then return the skillet to the heat, and bring to a boil,
stirring constantly. Stir in the cooking apple, bay leaves,
and honey, and season to taste with salt and pepper.

4 Pour the mixture over the chicken, cover and cook on
low for 6½ hours, until the chicken is tender and the
juices run clear when the thickest part is pierced with
a sharp knife. Stir in the yellow bell pepper, re-cover,
and cook on high for 45 minutes.

5 Preheat the broiler. Brush the apple slices with the
melted butter and sprinkle them with sugar. Broil
for 2–3 minutes on each side until the sugar has
caramelized. Serve the stew garnished with the
caramelized apple slices and the mint.

turkey hash

ingredients

serves 4

1 tbsp olive oil
1 lb 2 oz/500 g ground turkey
1 large red onion, diced
1 lb 4 oz/550 g butternut squash,
    peeled, seeded, and diced
2 celery stalks, sliced
2 large potatoes, peeled and diced
3 tbsp Worcestershire sauce
2 bay leaves
salt and pepper

method

1 Preheat the slow cooker, if necessary, or according
   to the manufacturer's directions.

2 Heat the oil in a skillet, add the turkey, and sauté over
   high heat, stirring, until broken up and lightly browned
   all over.

3 Place all the vegetables in the slow cooker, then add
   the turkey and pan juices. Add the Worcestershire
   sauce and bay leaves and season with salt and pepper.
   Cover and cook on low for 7 hours. Serve in warmed
   bowls.

turkey & rice casserole

ingredients

serves 4

1 tbsp olive oil
1 lb 2 oz/500 g diced
    turkey breast
1 onion, diced
2 carrots, diced
2 celery stalks, sliced
3½ cups sliced closed-cup
    mushrooms
1 cup long-grain rice,
    preferably Basmati
2 cups hot chicken stock
salt and pepper

method

1 Preheat the slow cooker, if necessary, or according
   to the manufacturer's directions.

2 Heat the oil in a heavy skillet, add the turkey, and
   sauté over high heat for 3–4 minutes, until the turkey
   is lightly browned.

3 Combine the onion, carrots, celery, mushrooms, and
   rice in the slow cooker. Arrange the turkey on top,
   season well with salt and pepper, and pour the stock
   over. Cover and cook on high for 2 hours.

4 Stir lightly with a fork to mix, adjust the seasoning
   to taste, and serve immediately

turkey pasta casserole

ingredients

serves 4

9 oz/250 g dried macaroni
¾ cup tomato juice
1 lb 2 oz/500 g ground turkey
1 small onion, finely chopped
1 cup fresh white breadcrumbs
3½ fl oz/100 ml pesto sauce
4½ oz/125 g mozzarella cheese
salt and pepper
fresh basil leaves, to garnish

method

1 Preheat the slow cooker, if necessary, or according to the manufacturer's directions.

2 Bring a large saucepan of lightly salted water to a boil, add the pasta, return to a boil, and cook for half the amount of time stated on the package. Drain well, place in the slow cooker, and stir in the tomato juice.

3 Mix the turkey, onion, and breadcrumbs together. Season well with salt and pepper. Divide the mixture into about 20 small balls, rolling them with your hands.

4 Arrange the meatballs over the pasta in a single layer and spoon a little of the pesto sauce on top of each. Cover and cook on high for 2 hours.

5 Tear the mozzarella cheese into small pieces and scatter over the meatballs. Cover and cook on high for an additional 20 minutes. Serve immediately, garnished with fresh basil.

pot roast with beer

ingredients

serves 4–6

2 small onions, each cut into
    8 wedges
8 small carrots, halved lengthwise
1 fennel bulb, cut into 8 wedges
5 lb/2.25 kg rolled chuck steak
2 tbsp Dijon mustard
1 tbsp all-purpose flour
scant $\frac{1}{2}$ cup beer
salt and pepper

method

1 Preheat the slow cooker, if necessary, or according
  to the manufacturer's directions.

2 Place the onions, carrots, and fennel in the slow cooker
  and season to taste with salt and pepper. Place the
  beef on top.

3 Mix the mustard and flour together to form a paste and
  spread over the beef. Season well and pour over the
  beer. Cover and cook on low for 8 hours.

4 Carefully remove the beef and vegetables and place
  on a warmed platter. Skim the excess fat from the
  juices and pour into a pitcher to serve with the beef.

spicy beef

ingredients

serves 4

1½ tbsp all-purpose flour
1 lb/450 g braising beef,
    cut into 1-inch/2.5 cm cubes
2 tbsp olive oil
1 red onion, sliced
3–4 garlic cloves, crushed
1 green chile, seeded and chopped
3 celery stalks, sliced
4 cloves
1 tsp ground allspice
1–2 tsp hot pepper sauce
2½ cups beef stock
1¾ cups chopped peeled acorn
    or other squash
1 large red bell pepper,
    seeded and chopped
4 tomatoes, coarsely chopped
4 oz/115 g okra, trimmed
    and halved
mixed wild and long-grain rice,
    to serve

method

1 Preheat the slow cooker, if necessary, or according to the manufacturer's directions.

2 Spread out the flour in a shallow dish, add the beef cubes, and toss until well coated. Shake off any excess and reserve the remaining flour.

3 Heat the oil in a heavy skillet. Add the onion, garlic, chile, celery, cloves, and allspice and cook over low heat, stirring occasionally, for 5 minutes, until the vegetables have softened. Increase the heat to high, add the beef cubes, and cook, stirring frequently, for 3 minutes, until browned all over. Sprinkle in the reserved flour and cook, stirring constantly, for 2 minutes, then remove the skillet from the heat.

4 Stir in the hot pepper sauce, then gradually stir in the stock. Return the skillet to the heat and bring to a boil, stirring constantly. Transfer the mixture to the slow cooker and add the squash. Cover and cook on low for 8 hours.

5 Add the red bell pepper, tomatoes, and okra, re-cover, and cook on high for 1 hour. Serve with mixed wild and long-grain rice.

beef & pearl onion casserole

ingredients

serves 4-6

2 tbsp olive oil

1 lb/450 g pearl onions,
    peeled but left whole

2 garlic cloves, halved

2 lb/900 g braising beef, cubed

½ tsp ground cinnamon

1 tsp ground cloves

1 tsp ground cumin

2 tbsp tomato paste

3 cups red wine

grated rind and juice of 1 orange

1 bay leaf

salt and pepper

1 tbsp chopped fresh flat-leaf
    parsley, to garnish

boiled potatoes, to serve

method

1 Preheat the slow cooker, if necessary, or according
   to the manufacturer's directions.

2 Heat the oil in a heavy skillet. Add the onions and garlic
   and cook over medium heat, stirring frequently, for
   5 minutes, until softened and beginning to brown.
   Increase the heat to high, add the beef, and cook,
   stirring frequently, for 5 minutes, until browned all over.

3 Stir in the cinnamon, cloves, cumin, and tomato paste,
   and season with salt and pepper. Pour in the wine,
   scraping up any sediment from the base of the skillet.
   Stir in the orange rind and juice, add the bay leaf, and
   bring to a boil.

4 Transfer the mixture to the slow cooker, cover and
   cook on low for 9 hours, until the beef is tender.
   If possible, stir the stew once during the second half
   of the cooking time.

5 Serve the stew garnished with the parsley and
   accompanied by boiled potatoes.

beef stew with olives

ingredients

serves 4-6

2 lb/900 g braising beef, cubed
2 onions, thinly sliced
2 carrots, sliced
4 large garlic cloves, lightly
    crushed
1 bouquet garni
4 juniper berries
2¼ cups dry red wine
2 tbsp brandy
2 tbsp olive oil
3 tbsp all-purpose flour
⅔ cup lardons or diced bacon
2 x 4-inch strips of thinly pared
    orange rind
¾ cup pitted black olives, rinsed
salt and pepper
1 tbsp chopped fresh flat-leaf
    parsley and finely grated
    orange rind, to garnish
buttered noodles or tagliatelle,
    to serve

method

1 Preheat the slow cooker, if necessary, or according
   to the manufacturer's directions.

2 Put the beef in a large, nonmetallic dish. Add the
   onions, carrots, garlic, bouquet garni, and juniper
   berries, and season with salt and pepper. Combine
   the wine, brandy, and olive oil in a pitcher and pour
   over the meat and vegetables. Cover with plastic wrap
   and marinate in the refrigerator for 24 hours.

3 Using a slotted spoon, remove the beef from the
   marinade and pat dry with paper towels. Reserve the
   marinade, vegetables, and flavorings. Place the flour in
   a shallow dish and season well with salt and pepper.
   Toss the beef cubes in the flour until well coated and
   shake off any excess.

4 Sprinkle half the lardons in the base of the slow cooker
   and top with the beef cubes. Pour in the marinade,
   including the vegetables and flavorings, and add the
   strips of orange rind and the olives. Top with the
   remaining lardons. Cover and cook on low for 9½–10
   hours, until the beef and vegetables are tender.

5 Remove and discard the bouquet garni and skim
   off any fat that has risen to the surface of the stew.
   Sprinkle the parsley and grated rind over the top and
   serve with buttered noodles or tagliatelle.

goulash

ingredients

serves 4

4 tbsp sunflower oil
1 lb 7 oz/650 g braising beef,
   cut into 1-inch/2.5 cm cubes
2 tsp all-purpose flour
2 tsp paprika
1½ cups beef stock
3 onions, chopped
4 carrots, diced
1 large potato or 2 medium
   potatoes, diced
1 bay leaf
½–1 tsp caraway seeds
14 oz/400 g canned chopped
   tomatoes
2 tbsp sour cream
salt and pepper

method

1 Preheat the slow cooker, if necessary, or according
   to the manufacturer's directions.

2 Heat half the oil in a heavy skillet. Add the beef and
   cook over medium heat, stirring frequently, until
   browned all over. Lower the heat and stir in the flour
   and paprika. Cook, stirring constantly, for 2 minutes.
   Gradually stir in the stock and bring to a boil, then
   transfer the mixture to the slow cooker.

3 Rinse out the skillet and heat the remaining oil in it.
   Add the onions and cook over low heat, stirring
   occasionally, for 5 minutes until softened. Stir in the
   carrots and potato and cook for a few minutes more.
   Add the bay leaf, caraway seeds, and tomatoes with
   their can juices. Season with salt and pepper.

4 Transfer the vegetable mixture to the slow cooker, stir
   well, then cover, and cook on low for 9 hours until the
   meat is tender.

5 Remove and discard the bay leaf. Pour over the sour
   cream and serve immediately.

variation

For a slightly sweeter spice, substitute 1 teaspoon of
paprika for sweet paprika and add 1 teaspoon of sugar.

lamb with red bell peppers

ingredients

serves 4

1½ tbsp all-purpose flour
1 tsp ground cloves
1 lb/450 g boneless lamb,
    cut into thin strips
1–1½ tbsp olive oil
1 white onion, sliced
2–3 garlic cloves, sliced
1¼ cups orange juice
⅔ cup lamb or chicken stock
1 cinnamon stick
2 red bell peppers, seeded and
    sliced into rings
4 tomatoes
4 fresh cilantro sprigs
salt and pepper
1 tbsp chopped fresh cilantro,
    to garnish
mashed sweet potatoes mixed
    with chopped scallions and
    green vegetables, to serve

method

1 Preheat the slow cooker, if necessary, or according
   to the manufacturer's directions.

2 Combine the flour and ground cloves in a shallow dish,
   add the strips of lamb, and toss well to coat, shaking
   off any excess. Reserve the remaining spiced flour.

3 Heat 1 tablespoon of the oil in a heavy skillet, add the
   lamb, and cook over high heat, stirring frequently, for
   3 minutes, until browned all over. Using a slotted
   spoon, transfer the lamb to the slow cooker. Add the
   onion and garlic to the skillet, with the remaining oil if
   necessary, and cook over low heat, stirring occasionally,
   for 5 minutes, until softened. Sprinkle in the reserved
   spiced flour and cook, stirring constantly, for 2 minutes,
   then remove the skillet from the heat. Gradually stir
   in the orange juice and stock, then return the skillet
   to the heat, and bring to a boil, stirring constantly.

4 Pour the mixture over the lamb, add the cinnamon
   stick, bell peppers, tomatoes, and cilantro sprigs, and
   stir well. Cover and cook on low for 7–8 hours, until
   the meat is tender. Remove and discard the cinnamon
   stick and cilantro sprigs. Season to taste with salt
   and pepper, sprinkle the stew with chopped cilantro,
   and serve with mashed sweet potatoes with scallions
   and green vegetables.

ham with black-eyed peas

ingredients

serves 4

2–3 tbsp olive oil
1 lb 4 oz/550 g country-cured
    ham, trimmed and cut into
    1½-inch/4-cm pieces
1 onion, chopped
2–3 garlic cloves, chopped
2 celery stalks, chopped
6 oz/175 g carrots, thinly sliced
1 cinnamon stick
½ tsp ground cloves
¼ tsp freshly grated nutmeg
1 tsp dried oregano
2 cups chicken or vegetable stock
2 tbsp maple syrup
8 oz/225 g chorizo or other spicy
    sausages, skinned
14 oz/400 g canned black-eyed
    peas, drained and rinsed
1 orange bell pepper,
    seeded and chopped
1 tbsp cornstarch
pepper
fresh flat-leaf parsley or
    oregano sprig, to garnish

method

1 Preheat the slow cooker, if necessary, or according to the manufacturer's directions.

2 Heat 1 tablespoon of the oil in a heavy skillet, add the ham, and cook over high heat, stirring frequently, for 5 minutes, until browned all over. Using a slotted spoon, transfer the ham to the slow cooker.

3 Add 1 tablespoon of the remaining oil to the skillet. Reduce the heat to low, add the onion, garlic, celery, and carrots, and cook, stirring occasionally, for 5 minutes, until softened. Add the cinnamon, cloves, and nutmeg, season with pepper, and cook, stirring constantly, for 2 minutes. Stir in the dried oregano, stock, and maple syrup and bring to a boil, stirring constantly. Pour the mixture over the ham, stir well, cover, and cook on low for 5–6 hours.

4 Heat the remaining oil in a skillet, add the chorizo, and cook for 10 minutes, until browned all over. Remove from the skillet, cut each into 3–4 chunks, and add to the slow cooker with the black-eyed peas and bell pepper. Re-cover and cook on high for 1–1½ hours. Stir the cornstarch with 2 tablespoons water to a smooth paste in a small bowl, then stir into the stew, re-cover, and cook on high for 15 minutes. Discard the cinnamon stick, garnish the stew with a fresh herb sprig, and serve.

tagliatelle with shrimp

ingredients

serves 4

14 oz/400 g tomatoes,
    peeled and chopped
5 oz/140 g tomato paste
1 garlic clove, finely chopped
2 tbsp chopped fresh parsley
1 lb 2 oz/500 g cooked, peeled
    large shrimp
6 fresh basil leaves, torn
14 oz/400 g dried tagliatelle
salt and pepper
fresh basil leaves, to garnish

method

1 Preheat the slow cooker, if necessary, or according
   to the manufacturer's directions.

2 Put the tomatoes, tomato paste, garlic, and parsley
   in the slow cooker and season with salt and pepper.
   Cover and cook on low for 7 hours.

3 Add the shrimp and basil. Re-cover and cook on high
   for 15 minutes.

4 Meanwhile, bring a large pan of lightly salted water to
   a boil. Add the pasta, bring back to a boil, and cook for
   10–12 minutes until tender but still firm to the bite.

5 Drain the pasta and tip it into a warmed serving bowl.
   Add the shrimp sauce and toss lightly with 2 large
   forks. Garnish with the basil and serve immediately.

spicy seafood & okra

ingredients

serves 6

2 tbsp sunflower or corn oil
6 oz/175 g okra, trimmed and cut
    into 1-inch/2.5-cm pieces
2 onions, finely chopped
4 celery stalks, very finely chopped
1 garlic clove, finely chopped
2 tbsp all-purpose flour
½ tsp sugar
1 tsp ground cumin
3 cups fish stock
1 red bell pepper, seeded
    and chopped
1 green bell pepper,
    seeded and chopped
2 large tomatoes, chopped
4 tbsp chopped fresh parsley
1 tbsp chopped fresh cilantro
dash of Tabasco
12 oz/350 g oz raw jumbo shrimp,
    peeled and deveined
12 oz/350 g cod or haddock fillet,
    skinned and cut into 1-inch/
    2.5 cm chunks
12 oz/350 g monkfish fillet,
    cut into 1-inch/2.5 cm chunks
salt and pepper

method

1 Preheat the slow cooker, if necessary, or according
   to the manufacturer's directions.

2 Heat half the oil in a heavy skillet. Add the okra and
   cook over low heat, stirring frequently, for 5 minutes,
   until browned. Using a slotted spoon, transfer the okra
   to the slow cooker.

3 Add the remaining oil to the skillet. Add the onions
   and celery, and cook over low heat, stirring occasionally,
   for 5 minutes, until softened. Add the garlic and cook,
   stirring frequently, for 1 minute, then sprinkle in the
   flour, sugar, and cumin, and season with salt and
   pepper. Cook, stirring constantly for 2 minutes, then
   remove the skillet from the heat.

4 Gradually stir in the stock, then return the skillet to the
   heat, and bring to a boil, stirring constantly. Pour the
   mixture over the okra and stir in the bell peppers and
   tomatoes. Cover and cook on low for 5–6 hours.

5 Stir in the parsley, cilantro, and Tabasco to taste, then
   add the shrimp, cod, and monkfish. Cover and cook
   on high for 30 minutes, until the fish and shrimp are
   ready. Taste and adjust the seasoning if necessary
   and serve.

green chilli seafood stew

ingredients
serves 4

2 tbsp olive oil, plus extra
for drizzling
1 large onion, chopped
4 garlic cloves, finely chopped
1 yellow bell pepper, seeded,
and chopped
1 red bell pepper, seeded,
and chopped
1 orange bell pepper, seeded,
and chopped
1 lb/450 g tomatoes, peeled
and chopped
2 large, mild green chiles,
such as poblano, chopped
finely grated rind and juice
of 1 lime
2 tbsp chopped fresh cilantro,
plus extra leaves to garnish
1 bay leaf
2 cups fish, vegetable,
or chicken stock
1 lb/450 g red snapper
1 lb/450 g raw shrimp
8 oz/225 g cleaned squid
salt and pepper

method

1 Preheat the slow cooker, if necessary, or according
to the manufacturer's directions.

2 Heat the oil in a pan. Add the onion and garlic and
cook over low heat, stirring occasionally, for 5 minutes,
until softened. Add the bell peppers, tomatoes, and
chiles and cook, stirring frequently, for 5 minutes. Stir
in the grated lime rind and juice, add the chopped
cilantro and bay leaf, and pour in the stock. Bring to
a boil, stirring occasionally.

3 Transfer the mixture to the slow cooker, cover, and
cook on low for 7½ hours. Meanwhile, skin the fish
fillets, if necessary, and cut the flesh into chunks. Peel
and devein the shrimp. Cut the squid bodies into
rings and halve the tentacles or leave them whole.

4 Add the seafood to the stew, season with salt and
pepper, re-cover, and cook on high for 30 minutes,
or until the seafood is tender and cooked through.
Remove and discard the bay leaf, garnish the stew
with cilantro leaves, and serve.

tagliatelle with tuna

ingredients

serves 4

7 oz/200 g dried egg tagliatelle
14 oz/400 g canned tuna steak
   in oil, drained
1 bunch scallions, sliced
1¼ cups frozen peas
2 tsp hot chili sauce
1¼ cups hot chicken stock
1 cup grated cheddar cheese
salt and pepper

method

1 Preheat the slow cooker, if necessary, or according to the manufacturer's directions.

2 Bring a large saucepan of lightly salted water to a boil. Add the pasta, return to a boil, and cook for 2 minutes, until the pasta ribbons are loose. Drain.

3 Break up the tuna into bite-size chunks and place in the slow cooker with the pasta, scallions, and peas. Season to taste with salt and pepper.

4 Add the chili sauce to the stock and pour over the ingredients in the slow cooker. Sprinkle the grated cheese over the top. Cover and cook on low for 2 hours. Serve immediately in warmed bowls.

spring vegetables

ingredients

serves 4

2 tbsp olive oil

4–8 pearl onions, halved

2 celery stalks, cut into
 ¼-inch/5-mm slices

8 oz/225 g young carrots, halved
 if large

10½ oz/300 g new potatoes,
 halved

4–5 cups vegetable stock

1¼ cups dried cannellini beans,
 soaked overnight in cold water
 and drained

1 bouquet garni

1½–2 tbsp light soy sauce

¾ cup baby corn

⅔ cup shelled fava beans,
 thawed if frozen

2½ cups shredded Savoy cabbage

1½ tbsp cornstarch

salt and pepper

⅔–1 cup freshly grated
 Parmesan cheese, to serve

method

1 Preheat the slow cooker, if necessary, or according
 to the manufacturer's directions.

2 Heat the oil in a pan. Add the onions, celery, carrots,
 and potatoes and cook over low heat, stirring
 frequently, for 5–8 minutes, until softened. Add the
 stock, cannellini beans, bouquet garni, and soy sauce,
 bring to a boil, then transfer to the slow cooker.

3 Add the corn, fava beans, and cabbage, season with
 salt and pepper, and stir well. Cover and cook on high
 for 3–4 hours, until the vegetables are tender.

4 Remove and discard the bouquet garni. Stir the
 cornstarch with 3 tablespoons water to a paste in a
 small bowl, then stir into the stew. Re-cover and cook
 on high for a further 15 minutes, until thickened. Serve
 the stew with the Parmesan handed separately.

slow cooked vegetables with parsley dumplings

ingredients

serves 6

½ rutabaga, cut into chunks
2 onions, sliced
2 potatoes, cut into chunks
2 carrots, cut into chunks
2 celery stalks, sliced
2 zucchini, sliced
2 tbsp tomato paste
2½ cups hot vegetable stock
1 bay leaf
1 tsp ground coriander
½ tsp dried thyme
salt and pepper
parsley sprigs, to garnish

parsley dumplings

1¾ cups self-rising flour
⅔ cup vegetable shortening
2 tbsp chopped fresh parsley
½ cup milk

method

1 Preheat the slow cooker, if necessary, or according to the manufacturer's directions.

2 Put the rutabaga, onions, potatoes, carrots, celery, and zucchini into the slow cooker. Stir the tomato paste into the stock and pour it over the vegetables. Add the bay leaf, ground coriander, and thyme and season with salt and pepper. Cover and cook on low for 6 hours.

3 To make the dumplings, sift the flour with a pinch of salt into a bowl and rub in the shortening and parsley. Add just enough milk to make a firm but light dough. Knead lightly and shape into 12 small balls.

4 Place the dumplings on top of the vegetables. Cook on high for 30 minutes. Serve immediately, garnished with parsley.

winter vegetables

ingredients

serves 4

2 tbsp sunflower oil
2 onions, chopped
3 carrots, halved lengthwise
3 parsnips, halved lengthwise
2 bunches celery, cut into long
  chunks
2 tbsp chopped fresh parsley
1 tbsp chopped fresh cilantro
1¼ cups vegetable stock
salt and pepper

method

1 Preheat the slow cooker, if necessary, or according to the manufacturer's directions.

2 Heat the oil in a large, heavy pan. Add the onions and cook over medium heat, stirring occasionally, for 5 minutes until softened. Add the carrots, parsnips, and celery and cook, stirring occasionally, for 5 minutes more. Stir in the herbs, season with salt and pepper, and pour in the stock. Bring to a boil.

3 Transfer the vegetable mixture to the slow cooker, cover, and cook on high for 3 hours until tender. Taste and adjust the seasoning if necessary. Using a slotted spoon, transfer the vegetables to warmed plates, then spoon over a little of the cooking liquid and serve.

vegetables & lentils

ingredients

serves 4

1 onion
10 cloves
1 cup green lentils
1 bay leaf
6¾ cups hot vegetable stock
2 leeks, sliced
2 potatoes, diced
2 carrots, chopped
3 zucchini, sliced
1 celery stalk, sliced
1 red bell pepper, seeded
    and chopped
1 tbsp lemon juice
salt and pepper

method

1 Preheat the slow cooker, if necessary, or according to the manufacturer's directions.

2 Peel the onion, stud it with the cloves and place it in the slow cooker. Add the lentils and bay leaf, pour in the stock, cover, and cook on high for 1½–2 hours.

3 Remove the onion with a slotted spoon and re-cover the slow cooker. Remove and discard the cloves and slice the onion. Add the onion, leeks, potatoes, carrots, zucchini, celery, and red bell pepper to the lentils, season with salt and pepper, re-cover, and cook on high for 3–4 hours, until all the vegetables are tender.

4 Remove and discard the bay leaf and stir in the lemon juice. Taste and adjust the seasoning if necessary, then serve.

baked eggplant with zucchini & tomato

ingredients

serves 4

2 large eggplants
olive oil, for brushing
2 large zucchini, sliced
4 tomatoes, sliced
1 garlic clove, finely chopped
2½ tbsp dry breadcrumbs
2½ tbsp grated Parmesan cheese
salt and pepper
freshly torn basil leaves, to garnish

method

1 Preheat the slow cooker, if necessary, or according to the manufacturer's directions.

2 Cut the eggplants into fairly thin slices and brush with oil. Heat a large grill pan or heavy skillet over high heat, then add the eggplants and cook in batches for 6–8 minutes, turning once, until soft and brown.

3 Layer the eggplants in the slow cooker with the zucchini, tomatoes, and garlic, seasoning with salt and pepper between the layers.

4 Mix the breadcrumbs with the cheese and sprinkle over the vegetables. Cover and cook on low for 4 hours. Serve hot, garnished with basil.

four bean chili

ingredients

serves 4–6

2 tbsp olive oil

1 onion, chopped

2–4 garlic cloves, chopped

2 red chiles, seeded and chopped

1²/₃ cups drained canned red
    kidney beans, rinsed

1¹/₃ cups drained canned
    garbanzo beans, rinsed

1²/₃ cups drained canned
    cannellini beans, rinsed

1 tbsp tomato paste

3 cups vegetable stock

1 red bell pepper, seeded and
    chopped

4 tomatoes, coarsely chopped

generous 1 cup shelled fava beans,
    thawed if frozen

1 tbsp chopped fresh cilantro

sour cream, to serve

fresh cilantro sprigs and pinch
    of paprika, to garnish

method

1 Preheat the slow cooker, if necessary, or according
   to the manufacturer's directions.

2 Heat the oil in a heavy skillet. Add the onion, garlic,
   and chiles and cook over low heat, stirring occasionally,
   for 5 minutes, until softened. Add the kidney beans,
   garbanzo beans, and cannellini beans. Combine the
   tomato paste with a little of the stock in a pitcher and
   pour it over the beans. Add the remaining stock and
   bring to a boil.

3 Transfer the mixture to the slow cooker, cover, and
   cook on low for 3 hours. Stir in the bell pepper,
   tomatoes, fava beans, and chopped cilantro, re-cover,
   and cook on high for 1–1¹/₂ hours, until all the beans
   are tender.

4 Serve the stew topped with spoonfuls of sour cream
   and garnished with cilantro sprigs and a sprinkling
   of paprika.

entertaining

chunky beef chili

ingredients

serves 4

1¹/₃ cups dried red kidney beans,
    soaked overnight
2¹/₂ cups cold water
2 garlic cloves, chopped
¹/₃ cup tomato paste
1 small green chile, chopped
2 tsp ground cumin
2 tsp ground coriander
1 lb 5 oz/600 g chuck steak, diced
1 large onion, chopped
1 large green bell pepper,
    seeded and sliced
salt and pepper
sour cream, to serve

method

1 Preheat the slow cooker, if necessary, or according
   to the manufacturer's directions.

2 Drain the beans and place in a saucepan, cover
   with cold water, and bring to a boil. Boil rapidly for
   10 minutes, then remove from the heat and drain.
   Place the beans in the slow cooker and add the cold
   water to cover.

3 Mix the garlic, tomato paste, chile, cumin, and
   coriander together in a large bowl. Add the steak,
   onion, and green pepper and mix to coat evenly.

4 Place the meat and vegetables on top of the beans,
   cover, and cook on low for 9 hours, until the beans and
   meat are tender.

5 Stir, season to taste with salt and pepper, and serve
   with sour cream.

traditional pot roast

ingredients

serves 4–6

1 onion, finely chopped
4 carrots, sliced
4 baby turnips, sliced
4 celery stalks, sliced
2 potatoes, peeled and sliced
1 sweet potato, peeled and sliced
3–4 lb/1.3–1.8 kg beef pot roast
1 bouquet garni
1¼ cups hot beef stock
salt and pepper

method

1 Preheat the slow cooker, if necessary, or according to the manufacturer's directions.

2 Place the onion, carrots, turnips, celery, potatoes, and sweet potato in the slow cooker and stir to mix well.

3 Rub the beef all over with salt and pepper, then place on top of the bed of vegetables. Add the bouquet garni and pour in the stock. Cover and cook on low for 9–10 hours, until the beef is cooked to your liking.

4 Remove the beef, carve into slices, and arrange on serving plates. Spoon some of the vegetables and cooking juices onto the plates and serve.

duckling with apples

ingredients

serves 6

4–4 lb 8 oz/1.8–2 kg duckling,
cut into 8 pieces
2 tbsp olive oil
1 onion, finely chopped
1 carrot, finely chopped
1¼ cups chicken stock
1¼ cups dry white wine
bouquet garni
4 eating apples
¼ cup butter
salt and pepper

method

1 Preheat the slow cooker, if necessary, or according to the manufacturer's directions.

2 Season the duckling pieces with salt and pepper. Heat the oil in a large, heavy skillet. Add all the duckling pieces, placing the breast portions skin side down. Cook over medium–high heat for a few minutes until golden brown, then transfer the breast portions to a plate. Turn the other pieces and continue to cook until browned all over. Transfer to the plate.

3 Add the onion and carrot and cook over low heat, stirring occasionally, for 5 minutes until the onion is softened. Add the stock and wine and bring to a boil.

4 Transfer the vegetable mixture to the slow cooker. Add the duckling pieces and the bouquet garni. Cover and cook on low for 8 hours, occasionally skimming off the fat from the slow cooker and replacing the lid each time. Shortly before you are ready to serve, peel, core, and slice the apples. Melt the butter in a large skillet. Add the apple slices and cook over medium heat, turning occasionally, for 5 minutes until golden.

5 Spoon the cooked apples onto warmed plates and divide the duckling among them. Skim off the fat and strain the sauce into a pitcher, then pour it over the duckling, and serve.

Moroccan lamb casserole

ingredients

serves 6

3 tbsp olive oil

2 red onions, chopped

2 garlic cloves, finely chopped

1-inch/2.5-cm piece fresh ginger, finely chopped

1 yellow bell pepper, seeded and chopped

2 lb 4 oz/1 kg boneless shoulder of lamb, trimmed and cut into 1-inch/2.5 cm cubes

3¾ cups lamb or chicken stock

1 cup plumped dried apricots, halved

1 tbsp honey

4 tbsp lemon juice

pinch of saffron threads

2-inch/5-cm cinnamon stick

salt and pepper

½ cup sliced almonds, toasted

fresh cilantro sprigs, to garnish

method

1 Preheat the slow cooker, if necessary, or according to the manufacturer's directions.

2 Heat the oil in a large, heavy pan. Add the onions, garlic, ginger, and bell pepper and cook over low heat, stirring occasionally, for 5 minutes until the onion has softened. Add the lamb and stir well to mix, then pour in the stock. Add the apricots, honey, lemon juice, saffron, and cinnamon stick, and season with the salt and pepper. Bring to a boil.

3 Transfer the mixture to the slow cooker. Cover and cook on low for 8½ hours until the meat is tender.

4 Remove and discard the cinnamon stick. Transfer to warmed serving bowls, sprinkle with the almonds, garnish with fresh cilantro, and serve.

springtime lamb with asparagus

ingredients

serves 6

2 tbsp sunflower oil
1 onion, thinly sliced
2 garlic cloves, very finely chopped
2 lb 4 oz/1 kg boneless shoulder
   of lamb, cut into 1-inch/
   2.5-cm cubes
8 oz/225 g asparagus spears,
   thawed if frozen
1¼ cups chicken stock
4 tbsp lemon juice
⅔ cup heavy cream
salt and pepper

method

1 Preheat the slow cooker, if necessary, or according
   to the manufacturer's directions.

2 Heat the oil in a large, heavy skillet. Add the onion
   and cook over medium heat, stirring occasionally, for
   5 minutes until softened. Add the garlic and lamb and
   cook, stirring occasionally, for 5 minutes more until the
   lamb is lightly browned all over.

3 Meanwhile, trim off and reserve the tips of the
   asparagus spears. Cut the stalks into 2–3 pieces. Add
   the stock and lemon juice to the skillet, season with
   salt and pepper, and bring to a boil. Lower the heat,
   add the asparagus stalks, and simmer for 2 minutes.

4 Transfer the mixture to the slow cooker. Cover and
   cook on low for 7 hours until the lamb is tender.

5 About 20 minutes before you intend to serve, cook
   the reserved asparagus tips in a pan of lightly salted,
   boiling water for 5 minutes. Drain well, then combine
   with the cream. Spoon the cream mixture on top of the
   lamb mixture but do not stir it in. Re-cover and cook on
   high for 15–20 minutes to heat through before serving.

lamb shanks with olives

ingredients

serves 4

1½ tbsp all-purpose flour
4 lamb shanks
2 tbsp olive oil
1 onion, sliced
2 garlic cloves, finely chopped
2 tsp sweet paprika
14 oz/400 g canned chopped
    tomatoes
2 tbsp tomato paste
2 carrots, sliced
2 tsp sugar
1 cup red wine
2-inch/5-cm cinnamon stick
2 fresh rosemary sprigs
1 cup pitted black olives
2 tbsp lemon juice
2 tbsp chopped fresh mint
salt and pepper
fresh mint sprigs, to garnish

method

1 Preheat the slow cooker, if necessary, or according
   to the manufacturer's directions.

2 Spread out the flour on a plate and season with salt
   and pepper. Toss the lamb in the seasoned flour and
   shake off any excess. Heat the oil in a large, heavy pan.
   Add the lamb shanks and cook over medium heat,
   turning frequently, for 6–8 minutes until browned all
   over. Transfer to a plate and set aside.

3 Add the onion and garlic to the pan and cook, stirring
   frequently, for 5 minutes until softened. Stir in the
   paprika and cook for 1 minute. Add the tomatoes,
   tomato paste, carrots, sugar, wine, cinnamon stick,
   and rosemary and bring to a boil.

4 Transfer the vegetable mixture to the slow cooker
   and add the lamb shanks. Cover and cook on low
   for 8 hours until the lamb is very tender.

5 Add the olives, lemon juice, and mint to the slow
   cooker. Re-cover and cook on high for 30 minutes.
   Remove and discard the rosemary and cinnamon
   and serve, garnished with mint sprigs.

cinnamon lamb

ingredients

serves 6

2 tbsp all-purpose flour
2 lb 4 oz/1 kg lean boneless
    lamb, cubed
2 tbsp olive oil
2 large onions, sliced
1 garlic clove, finely chopped
1¼ cups red wine
2 tbsp red wine vinegar
14 oz/400 g canned chopped
    tomatoes
scant ½ cup raisins
1 tbsp ground cinnamon
pinch of sugar
1 bay leaf
⅔ cup plain strained yogurt
2 garlic cloves, crushed
salt and pepper
paprika, to garnish

method

1 Preheat the slow cooker, if necessary, or according
   to the manufacturer's directions.

2 Spread out the flour in a shallow dish and season with
   pepper. Add the lamb cubes and toss until well coated,
   shaking off any excess.

3 Heat the oil in a heavy skillet. Add the onions and
   garlic and cook over low heat, stirring occasionally,
   for 5 minutes, until softened. Increase the heat to
   high, add the lamb, and cook, stirring frequently, for
   5 minutes, until evenly browned.

4 Stir in the wine, vinegar, and tomatoes with their can
   juices, and bring to a boil, scraping up any sediment
   from the base of the skillet. Transfer to the slow cooker,
   stir in the raisins, cinnamon, sugar, and bay leaf, and
   season with salt and pepper. Cover and cook on low
   for 8–8½ hours, until the lamb is tender.

5 Meanwhile, prepare the topping. Combine the yogurt
   and garlic in a small bowl and season to taste with salt
   and pepper. Cover and chill in the refrigerator until
   ready to serve.

6 Remove and discard the bay leaf. Serve each portion
   topped with a spoonful of the garlic-flavored yogurt
   garnished with a little paprika.

pork with almonds

ingredients

serves 4

2 tbsp corn or sunflower oil
2 onions, chopped
2 garlic cloves, finely chopped
2-inch/5-cm cinnamon stick
3 cloves
1 cup ground almonds
1 lb 10 oz/750 g boneless pork,
    cut into 1-inch/2.5-cm cubes
4 tomatoes, peeled and chopped
2 tbsp capers
1 cup green olives, pitted
3 pickled jalapeño chiles, drained,
    seeded, and cut into rings
1½ cups chicken stock
salt and pepper

method

1 Preheat the slow cooker, if necessary, or according
   to the manufacturer's directions.

2 Heat half the oil in a large, heavy skillet. Add the
   onions and cook over low heat, stirring occasionally,
   for 5 minutes until softened. Add the garlic, cinnamon,
   cloves, and almonds and cook, stirring frequently, for
   8–10 minutes. Be careful not to burn the almonds.

3 Remove and discard the spices and transfer the
   mixture to a food processor. Process the mixture to
   a smooth puree.

4 Rinse out the skillet and return to the heat. Heat
   the remaining oil, then add the pork, in batches if
   necessary. Cook over medium heat, stirring frequently,
   for 5–10 minutes until browned all over. Return all
   the pork to the skillet and add the almond puree,
   tomatoes, capers, olives, chiles, and chicken stock.
   Bring to a boil, then transfer to the slow cooker.

5 Season with salt and pepper and mix well. Cover and
   cook on low for 5 hours. To serve, transfer to warmed
   plates and serve immediately.

pork & vegetable ragout

ingredients

serves 4

1 lb/450 g lean, boneless pork
1½ tbsp all-purpose flour
1 tsp ground coriander
1 tsp ground cumin
1½ tsp ground cinnamon
1 tbsp olive oil
1 onion, chopped
14 oz/400 g canned chopped
   tomatoes
2 tbsp tomato paste
1¼ cups chicken stock
1¼ cups chopped carrots
2⅔ cups chopped squash,
   such as kabocha
2 cups sliced leeks, blanched
   and drained
4 oz/115 g okra, trimmed
   and sliced
salt and pepper
fresh parsley sprigs, to garnish
couscous, to serve

method

1 Preheat the slow cooker, if necessary, or according to the manufacturer's directions.

2 Trim off any visible fat from the pork and cut the meat into thin strips about 2 inches long. Combine the flour, coriander, cumin, and cinnamon in a shallow dish, add the pork strips, and toss well to coat. Shake off the excess and reserve the remaining spiced flour.

3 Heat the oil in a heavy skillet. Add the onion and cook over low heat, stirring occasionally, for 5 minutes, until softened. Add the pork strips, increase the heat to high, and cook, stirring frequently, for 5 minutes, until browned all over. Sprinkle in the reserved spiced flour and cook, stirring constantly, for 2 minutes, then remove the skillet from the heat.

4 Gradually stir in the tomatoes with their can juices. Combine the tomato paste with the stock in a pitcher, then gradually stir the mixture into the skillet. Add the carrots, return the skillet to the heat, and bring to a boil, stirring constantly.

5 Transfer to the slow cooker, stir in the squash, leeks, and okra, and season with salt and pepper. Cover and cook on low for 5–6 hours, until the meat and vegetables are tender. Garnish with parsley sprigs and serve with couscous.

spicy pulled pork

ingredients

serves 4

2 onions, sliced
3 lb 5 oz/1.5 kg boned and rolled
    pork shoulder
2 tbsp raw brown sugar
2 tbsp Worcestershire sauce
1 tbsp mustard
2 tbsp ketchup
1 tbsp cider vinegar
salt and pepper
hamburger buns or ciabatta rolls,
    to serve

method

1 Preheat the slow cooker, if necessary, or according
   to the manufacturer's directions.

2 Put the onions in the slow cooker and place the pork
   on top. Mix the sugar, Worcestershire sauce, mustard,
   ketchup, and vinegar together and spread all over the
   surface of the pork. Season to taste with salt and
   pepper. Cover and cook on low for 8 hours.

3 Remove the pork from the slow cooker and use 2 forks
   to pull it apart into shreds.

4 Skim any excess fat from the juices and stir a little juice
   into the pork. Serve in hamburger buns, with the
   remaining juices for spooning over.

maple-glazed pork ribs

ingredients

serves 4

1 onion, finely chopped

2 plum tomatoes, diced

3 tbsp maple syrup

2 tbsp soy sauce

2 tsp hot chili sauce

3 lb 5 oz/1.5 kg meaty pork ribs,
   cut into single ribs

salt and pepper

method

1 Preheat the slow cooker, if necessary, or according to the manufacturer's directions.

2 Combine the onion, tomatoes, maple syrup, soy sauce, chili sauce, and salt and pepper to taste in a large bowl. Add the pork ribs and turn to coat evenly.

3 Arrange the ribs in the slow cooker, cover, and cook on high for 4 hours. If possible, turn the ribs halfway through the cooking time.

4 Lift out the ribs and place on a warmed platter. Skim the excess fat from the juices and spoon the juices over the ribs to serve.

slow roast chicken

ingredients

serves 4–6

3 lb 5 oz/1.5 kg chicken
½ lemon
1 tbsp olive oil
½ tsp dried thyme
½ tsp paprika
salt and pepper

method

1 Preheat the slow cooker, if necessary, or according to the manufacturer's directions.

2 Wipe the chicken with paper towels and tuck the ½ lemon inside the body cavity. Brush the oil over the chicken skin and sprinkle with thyme, paprika, and salt and pepper, rubbing in with your fingers to cover all the skin.

3 Place the chicken in the slow cooker, cover, and cook on high for 3 hours. Reduce the heat to low and cook for an additional 4 hours, until the chicken is tender and the juices run clear when a skewer is inserted into the thickest part of the meat.

4 Carefully remove the chicken and place on a warmed platter, then skim any fat from the juices. Adjust the seasoning to taste and serve.

nutty chicken

ingredients

serves 4

3 tbsp sunflower oil
4 skinless chicken portions
2 shallots, chopped
1 tsp ground ginger
1 tbsp all-purpose flour
scant 2 cups beef stock
½ cup walnut pieces
grated rind of 1 lemon
2 tbsp lemon juice
1 tbsp molasses
salt and pepper
fresh watercress or mizuna sprigs,
    to garnish

method

1 Preheat the slow cooker, if necessary, or according
   to the manufacturer's directions.

2 Heat the oil in a large, heavy skillet. Season the chicken
   portions with salt and pepper and add to the skillet.
   Cook the chicken over medium heat, turning
   occasionally, for 5–8 minutes, until lightly golden
   all over. Transfer to the slow cooker.

3 Add the shallots to the skillet and cook, stirring
   occasionally, for 3–4 minutes until softened. Sprinkle
   in the ginger and flour and cook, stirring constantly,
   for 1 minute. Gradually stir in the stock and bring to a
   boil, stirring constantly. Lower the heat and simmer for
   1 minute, then stir in the nuts, lemon rind and juice,
   and molasses.

4 Pour the sauce over the chicken. Cover and cook on
   low for 6 hours until the chicken is cooked through
   and tender. Taste and adjust the seasoning if necessary.
   Transfer the chicken to warmed bowls, spoon some of
   the sauce over each portion, garnish with watercress
   sprigs, and serve immediately.

chicken cacciatore

ingredients

serves 4

3 tbsp olive oil
4 skinless chicken portions
2 onions, sliced
2 garlic cloves, finely chopped
14 oz/400 g canned chopped
    tomatoes
1 tbsp tomato paste
2 tbsp chopped fresh parsley
2 tsp fresh thyme leaves
²/₃ cup red wine
salt and pepper
fresh thyme sprigs, to garnish

method

1 Preheat the slow cooker, if necessary, or according to the manufacturer's directions.

2 Heat the oil in a heavy skillet. Add the chicken portions and cook over medium heat, turning occasionally, for 10 minutes until golden all over. Using a slotted spoon, transfer the chicken to the slow cooker.

3 Add the onions to the skillet and cook, stirring occasionally, for 5 minutes until softened and just turning golden. Add the garlic, tomatoes and their can juices, tomato paste, parsley, thyme, and wine. Season with salt and pepper and bring to a boil.

4 Pour the tomato mixture over the chicken pieces. Cover and cook on low for 5 hours until the chicken is tender and cooked through. Taste and adjust the seasoning if necessary, and serve, garnished with sprigs of thyme.

chicken in white wine

ingredients

serves 4–6

2 tbsp all-purpose flour
1 chicken, about 3 lb 8 oz/1.6 kg,
    cut into 8 pieces
¼ cup butter
1 tbsp sunflower oil
4 shallots, finely chopped
12 white mushrooms, sliced
2 tbsp brandy
2¼ cups white wine
generous 1 cup heavy cream
salt and pepper
chopped fresh flat-leaf parsley,
    to garnish

method

1 Preheat the slow cooker, if necessary, or according to the manufacturer's directions.

2 Put the flour in a shallow dish and season with salt and pepper. Toss the chicken pieces in the flour until well coated. Heat half the butter with the oil in a heavy skillet. Add the chicken pieces and cook over medium–high heat, turning frequently, for 10 minutes, until golden all over. Transfer the chicken to a plate.

3 Melt the remaining butter in the skillet. Add the shallots and mushrooms and cook over medium–high heat, stirring constantly, for 3 minutes, until lightly browned. Return the chicken to the skillet and remove it from the heat. Warm the brandy in a small ladle, ignite, and pour it over the chicken, shaking the skillet gently until the flames have died down.

4 Return the skillet to the heat and pour in the wine. Bring to a boil over low heat. Transfer to the slow cooker, cover, and cook on low for 5–6 hours, until the chicken is tender. Transfer the chicken to a serving dish and keep warm. Skim off any fat from the liquid surface and pour the liquid into a pan. Stir in the cream and bring just to a boil over low heat. Season to taste with salt and pepper and pour the sauce over the chicken. Sprinkle with chopped parsley and serve immediately.

barbecue chicken

ingredients

serves 4

8 skinless chicken drumsticks
    or thighs
3 tbsp tomato paste
2 tbsp honey
1 tbsp Worcestershire sauce
juice of ½ lemon
½ tsp crushed dried chiles
1 garlic clove, crushed
salt and pepper

method

1 Preheat the slow cooker, if necessary, or according to the manufacturer's directions.

2 Using a sharp knife, cut slashes into the thickest parts of the chicken flesh.

3 Mix the tomato paste, honey, Worcestershire sauce, lemon juice, chiles, and garlic together and season with salt and pepper. Add the chicken and toss well to coat evenly.

4 Arrange the chicken in the slow cooker, cover, and cook on high for 3 hours.

5 Remove the chicken with a slotted spoon. Skim any fat from the juices and spoon over the chicken to serve.

variation

Use a whole chicken if preferred. Clean the chicken inside and out with paper towels. Cook the chicken in butter in a large pan until brown all over. Brush over the barbecue sauce. Place in the slow cooker and cook on high for 3 hours.

seafood in saffron sauce

ingredients

serves 4

2 tbsp olive oil
1 onion, sliced
2 celery stalks, sliced
pinch of saffron threads
1 tbsp chopped fresh thyme
2 garlic cloves, finely chopped
1 lb 12 oz/800 g canned tomatoes,
    drained and chopped
¾ cup dry white wine
8¾ cups fish stock
8 oz/225 g live clams
8 oz/225 g live mussels
12 oz/350 g red snapper fillets
1 lb/450 g monkfish fillet
8 oz/225 g squid rings, thawed
    if frozen
2 tbsp shredded fresh basil leaves
salt and pepper

method

1 Preheat the slow cooker, if necessary, or according
   to the manufacturer's directions.

2 Heat the oil in a heavy pan. Add the onion, celery,
   saffron, thyme, and a pinch of salt and cook over
   low heat, stirring occasionally, for 5 minutes, until
   softened. Add the garlic and cook, stirring constantly,
   for 2 minutes.

3 Add the tomatoes, wine, and stock, season with salt
   and pepper, and bring to a boil, stirring constantly.
   Transfer the mixture to the slow cooker, cover, and
   cook on low for 5 hours.

4 Meanwhile, scrub the shellfish under cold running
   water and pull the "beards" off the mussels. Discard
   any with broken shells or that do not shut immediately
   when sharply tapped. Cut the snapper and monkfish
   fillets into bite-size chunks.

5 Add the pieces of fish, the shellfish, and the squid
   rings to the slow cooker, re-cover, and cook on high for
   30 minutes, until the clams and mussels have opened
   and the fish is cooked through. Discard any shellfish
   that remain closed. Stir in the basil and serve.

mediterranean shellfish stew

ingredients

serves 8

1 tbsp olive oil

²/₃ cup diced bacon

2 tbsp butter

2 shallots, chopped

2 leeks, sliced

2 celery stalks, chopped

2 potatoes, diced

1 lb 8 oz/675 g tomatoes, peeled, seeded, and chopped

3 tbsp chopped fresh parsley

3 tbsp snipped fresh chives, plus extra to garnish

1 bay leaf

1 fresh thyme sprig

6¼ cups fish stock

24 live mussels

24 live clams

1 lb/450 g porgy fillets

24 raw jumbo shrimp

salt and pepper

method

1 Preheat the slow cooker, if necessary, or according to the manufacturer's directions.

2 Heat the oil in a heavy pan. Add the bacon and cook, stirring frequently, for 5–8 minutes, until crisp. Using a slotted spoon, transfer to the slow cooker. Add the butter to the skillet and when it has melted, add the shallots, leeks, celery, and potatoes. Cook over low heat, stirring occasionally, for 5 minutes, until softened. Stir in the tomatoes, parsley, chives, bay leaf, and thyme, pour in the stock, and bring to a boil, stirring constantly. Pour the mixture into the slow cooker, cover, and cook on low for 7 hours.

3 Meanwhile, scrub the mussels and clams under cold running water and pull off the "beards" from the mussels. Discard any with broken shells or that do not shut immediately when sharply tapped. Cut the fish fillets into bite-size chunks. Peel and devein the shrimp.

4 Remove and discard the bay leaf and thyme sprig from the stew. Season with salt and pepper and add all the seafood. Re-cover and cook on high for 30 minutes. Discard any shellfish that remain closed. Serve garnished with extra chives.

french-style fish stew

ingredients

serves 4–6

1 prepared squid

2 lb/900 g mixed white fish

24 raw jumbo shrimp, peeled and deveined, reserving heads and shells, tied in cheesecloth

2 tbsp olive oil

1 large onion, finely chopped

1 fennel bulb, thinly sliced, feathery fronds reserved

2 large garlic cloves, crushed

4 tbsp Pernod

large pinch of saffron threads, freshly toasted

4 cups fish stock

2 large tomatoes, peeled, seeded, and diced, or 14 oz/400 g canned chopped tomatoes, drained

1 tbsp tomato paste

1 bay leaf

pinch of sugar

pinch of dried chile flakes (optional)

salt and pepper

method

1 Preheat the slow cooker, if necessary, or according to the manufacturer's directions.

2 Cut off and reserve the tentacles from the squid and slice the body into ¼-inch/5 mm rings. Place the seafood in a bowl, cover, and chill in the refrigerator until required.

3 Heat the oil in a heavy skillet. Add the onion and fennel and cook over low heat, stirring occasionally, for 5 minutes, until softened. Add the garlic and cook, stirring frequently, for 2 minutes. Remove the skillet from the heat. Heat the Pernod in a ladle or small saucepan, ignite, and pour it over the onion and fennel, gently shaking the skillet until the flames have died down.

4 Return the skillet to the heat, stir in the toasted saffron, stock, tomatoes, tomato paste, bay leaf, sugar, and chile flakes, if using, and season with salt and pepper. Bring to a boil, then transfer to the slow cooker, add the bag of shrimp shells, cover and cook on low for 6 hours.

5 Remove and discard the bag of shrimp shells and the bay leaf. Add the seafood to the slow cooker, cover, and cook on high for 30 minutes, until the fish flakes easily with the point of a knife. Serve garnished with the reserved fennel fronds.

tilapia casserole

ingredients

serves 4

1 tbsp olive oil
1 red onion, sliced
1 yellow bell pepper,
    seeded and sliced
4 tilapia fillets, about
    5 oz/140 g each
2 tomatoes, thinly sliced
8 pitted black olives, halved
1 garlic clove, thinly sliced
2 tsp balsamic vinegar
juice of 1 orange
salt and pepper

method

1 Preheat the slow cooker, if necessary, or according to the manufacturer's directions.

2 Heat the oil in a skillet, add the onion and yellow bell pepper and sauté over high heat for 3–4 minutes, stirring, until lightly browned. Transfer to the slow cooker, cover, and cook on high for 1 hour.

3 Arrange the fish fillets over the vegetables and season with salt and pepper. Arrange a layer of tomatoes and olives over the top and sprinkle with the garlic, vinegar, and salt and pepper. Pour over the orange juice, cover, and cook on high for an additional 1 hour. Serve immediately.

poached salmon with dill & lime

ingredients

serves 4

3 tbsp butter, melted
1 onion, thinly sliced
2 large potatoes, peeled and
     thinly sliced
scant ½ cup hot fish stock or water
4 pieces skinless salmon fillet,
     about 5 oz/140 g each
juice of 1 lime
2 tbsp chopped fresh dill
salt and pepper
lime wedges, to serve

method

1 Preheat the slow cooker, if necessary, or according to the manufacturer's directions.

2 Brush the bottom of the slow cooker with 1 tablespoon of the butter. Layer the onion and potatoes in the slow cooker, sprinkling with salt and pepper between the layers. Add the stock and dot with 1 tablespoon of the butter. Cover and cook on low for 3 hours.

3 Arrange the salmon over the vegetables in a single layer. Drizzle the lime juice over, sprinkle with dill and salt and pepper, and pour the remaining butter on top. Cover and cook on low for an additional 1 hour, until the fish flakes easily.

4 Serve the salmon and vegetables on warmed plates with the juices spooned over and lime wedges on the side to squeeze over.

baked asparagus & spinach risotto

ingredients

serves 4

2 tbsp olive oil
4 shallots, finely chopped
1½ cups risotto rice
1 garlic clove, crushed
scant ½ cup dry white wine
3½ cups hot chicken stock or
    vegetable stock
7 oz/200 g asparagus spears
7 oz/200 g baby spinach leaves
heaping ⅓ cup finely grated
    Parmesan cheese
salt and pepper

method

1 Preheat the slow cooker, if necessary, or according
   to the manufacturer's directions.

2 Heat the oil in a skillet, add the shallots, and sauté over
   medium heat, stirring, for 2–3 minutes. Add the rice
   and garlic and cook for an additional 2 minutes, stirring.
   Add the wine and let it boil for 30 seconds.

3 Transfer the rice mixture to the slow cooker, add the
   stock, and season to taste with salt and pepper. Cover
   and cook on high for 2 hours, or until most of the liquid
   is absorbed.

4 Cut the asparagus into 1¾-inch/4.5-cm lengths. Stir
   into the rice, then spread the spinach over the top.
   Replace the lid and cook on high for an additional
   30 minutes, until the asparagus is just tender and the
   spinach is wilted.

5 Stir in the spinach with the Parmesan cheese, then
   adjust the seasoning to taste and serve immediately
   in warmed bowls.

bean stew

ingredients

serves 4

1 large fennel bulb

2 tbsp olive oil

1 red onion, cut into small wedges

2–4 garlic cloves, sliced

1 green chile, seeded and chopped

1 eggplant, about 8 oz/225 g,
    cut into chunks

2 tbsp tomato paste

2 cups vegetable stock

1 lb/450 g tomatoes, sliced

1 tbsp balsamic vinegar

4 fresh oregano sprigs

14 oz/400 g canned borlotti beans,
    drained and rinsed

14 oz/400 g canned cannellini
    beans, drained and rinsed

1 yellow bell pepper, seeded and
    cut into small strips

1 zucchini, halved lengthwise
    and sliced

½ cup pitted black olives

salt and pepper

1 oz/25 g grated Parmesan cheese,
    to garnish

method

1 Preheat the slow cooker, if necessary, or according to the manufacturer's directions.

2 Trim the fennel bulb, reserving the feathery fronds, then cut the bulb into thin strips. Heat the oil in a heavy skillet. Add the fennel strips, onion, garlic, and chile and cook over low heat, stirring occasionally, for 5–8 minutes, until softened. Add the eggplant and cook, stirring frequently, for 5 minutes.

3 Combine the tomato paste and half the stock in a pitcher and add to the skillet. Pour in the remaining stock, add the tomatoes, vinegar, and oregano, and bring to a boil, stirring constantly.

4 Transfer the mixture to the slow cooker. Stir in the beans, yellow bell pepper, zucchini, and olives, and season with salt and pepper. Cover and cook on high for 3–4 hours, until all the vegetables are tender.

5 Taste and adjust the seasoning if necessary. Thinly shave the Parmesan over the top of the stew, garnish with the reserved fennel fronds, and serve.

mixed bean chili

ingredients

serves 4–6

2 tbsp corn oil

1 onion, chopped

1 garlic clove, finely chopped

1 fresh red chile,
    seeded and chopped

1 yellow bell pepper,
    seeded and chopped

1 tsp ground cumin

1 tbsp chili powder

²/₃ cup dried red kidney beans,
    soaked overnight, drained,
    and rinsed

²/₃ cup dried black beans, soaked
    overnight, drained, and rinsed

²/₃ cup dried pinto beans, soaked
    overnight, drained, and rinsed

4 cups vegetable stock

1 tbsp sugar

salt and pepper

chopped fresh cilantro, to garnish

method

1 Preheat the slow cooker, if necessary, or according
    to the manufacturer's directions.

2 Heat the oil in a large, heavy pan. Add the onion, garlic,
    chile, and bell pepper and cook over medium heat,
    stirring occasionally, for 5 minutes. Stir in the cumin
    and chili powder and cook, stirring, for 1–2 minutes.
    Add the drained beans and stock and bring to a boil.
    Boil vigorously for 15 minutes.

3 Transfer the mixture to the slow cooker, cover, and
    cook on low for 10 hours until the beans are tender.

4 Season the mixture with salt and pepper, then ladle
    about one-third into a bowl. Mash well with a potato
    masher, then return the mashed beans to the slow
    cooker, and stir in the sugar. Serve immediately,
    sprinkled with chopped fresh cilantro.

mixed vegetables

ingredients

serves 4

2 large potatoes, peeled
    and cubed
2 zucchini, cubed
2 red bell peppers, seeded
    and cubed
2 red onions, sliced
2 tsp mixed dried herbs
generous 1 cup hot vegetable stock
salt and pepper

method

1 Preheat the slow cooker, if necessary, or according
    to the manufacturer's directions.

2 Layer all the vegetables in the slow cooker, sprinkling
    with herbs and salt and pepper between the layers.

3 Pour over the stock. Cover and cook on low for 7 hours.
    Serve in warmed bowls.

around the world

chicken stew

ingredients

serves 6

4 lb/1.8 kg chicken portions
2 tbsp paprika
2 tbsp olive oil
2 tbsp butter
1 lb/450 g onions, chopped
2 yellow bell peppers,
    seeded and chopped
14 oz/400 g canned chopped
    tomatoes
1 cup dry white wine
2 cups chicken stock
1 tbsp Worcestershire sauce
½ tsp Tabasco sauce
1 tbsp finely chopped fresh
    parsley
2 tbsp all-purpose flour
11½ oz/325 g canned corn, drained
15 oz/425 g canned lima beans,
    drained and rinsed
salt
fresh parsley sprigs, to garnish

method

1 Preheat the slow cooker, if necessary, or according to the manufacturer's directions.

2 Season the chicken portions with salt and dust with the paprika. Heat the oil and butter in a heavy skillet. Add the chicken portions and cook over medium–high heat, turning frequently, for 10 minutes, until golden brown all over. Using a slotted spoon, transfer the chicken to the slow cooker.

3 Add the onions and bell peppers to the skillet, lower the heat, and cook, stirring occasionally, for 5 minutes, until softened. Add the tomatoes with their can juices, wine, stock, Worcestershire sauce, Tabasco sauce and chopped parsley and bring to a boil, stirring constantly. Pour the mixture over the chicken, cover, and cook on low for 5 hours.

4 Combine the flour and 4 tablespoons water to a paste in a small, heatproof bowl. Add a ladleful of the cooking liquid and mix well, then stir the mixture into the stew. Add the corn and lima beans, re-cover, and cook on high for 30 minutes, until the chicken is tender and cooked through. Serve garnished with parsley sprigs.

chipotle chicken

ingredients

serves 4

4–6 dried chipotle chiles
4 garlic cloves, unpeeled
1 small onion, chopped
14 oz/400 g canned chopped
    tomatoes
1¼ cups boiling chicken
    or vegetable stock
4 skinless chicken breasts
salt and pepper

method

1 Preheat the oven to 400°F/200°C. Place the chiles in a bowl and pour in just enough hot water to cover. Set aside to soak for 30 minutes. Meanwhile, place the unpeeled garlic cloves on a cookie sheet and roast in the oven for about 10 minutes until soft. Remove from the oven and let cool.

2 Drain the chiles, reserving ½ cup of the soaking water. Seed the chiles, if you like, and chop coarsely. Place the chiles and reserved soaking water in a blender or food processor and process to a puree. Peel and mash the garlic in a bowl.

3 Preheat the slow cooker, if necessary, or according to the manufacturer's directions. Place the chile puree, garlic, onion, and tomatoes in the slow cooker and stir in the stock. Season the chicken portions with salt and pepper and place them in the slow cooker. Cover and cook on low for about 5 hours until the chicken is tender and cooked through.

4 Lift the chicken out of the slow cooker with a slotted spoon, cover, and keep warm. Pour the cooking liquid into a pan and bring to a boil on the stove. Boil for 5–10 minutes until reduced. Place the chicken on warmed plates, spoon the sauce over it, and serve.

orange chicken

ingredients

serves 4

1½ tbsp all-purpose flour
1 lb/450 g skinless, boneless
    chicken, cut into bite-size
    pieces
1 tbsp olive oil
1 onion, cut into wedges
2 celery stalks, sliced
⅔ cup orange juice
1¼ cups chicken stock
1 tbsp light soy sauce
1–2 tsp honey
1 tbsp grated orange rind
1 orange bell pepper,
    seeded and chopped
8 oz/225 g zucchini, halved
    lengthwise and sliced
2 corn cobs, cut into chunks
1 orange, peeled and segmented
salt and pepper
1 tbsp chopped fresh parsley,
    to garnish

method

1 Preheat the slow cooker, if necessary, or according to the manufacturer's directions.

2 Spread out the flour in a shallow dish and season with salt and pepper. Add the chicken and toss well to coat, shaking off any excess. Reserve the remaining seasoned flour.

3 Heat the oil in a heavy skillet. Add the chicken and cook over high heat, stirring frequently, for 5 minutes, until golden brown all over. Using a slotted spoon, transfer the chicken to the slow cooker.

4 Add the onion and celery to the skillet, lower the heat and cook, stirring occasionally, for 5 minutes, until softened. Sprinkle in the reserved seasoned flour and cook, stirring constantly, for 2 minutes. Remove the skillet from the heat. Gradually stir in the orange juice, stock, soy sauce, and honey, then add the orange rind. Return the skillet to the heat and bring to a boil, stirring constantly.

5 Pour the mixture over the chicken and add the orange bell pepper, zucchini, and corn cobs. Cover and cook on low for 5 hours, until the chicken is tender and cooked through. Stir in the orange, re-cover, and cook on high for 15 minutes. Serve garnished with the parsley.

chicken italian-style

ingredients

serves 4

1 tbsp all-purpose flour
4 chicken portions, about
    6 oz/175 g each
2½ tbsp olive oil
8–12 shallots, halved if large
2–4 garlic cloves, sliced
1¾ cups chicken stock
¼ cup dry sherry
4 fresh thyme sprigs
4 oz/115 g cherry tomatoes
1 cup baby corn, halved
    lengthwise
2 slices white or whole-wheat
    bread, crusts removed, cubed
salt and pepper
1 tbsp chopped fresh thyme,
    to garnish

method

1 Preheat the slow cooker, if necessary, or according
    to the manufacturer's directions.

2 Spread out the flour in a shallow dish and season with
    salt and pepper. Add the chicken portions and toss well
    to coat, shaking off any excess. Reserve the remaining
    seasoned flour. Heat 1 tablespoon of the oil in a heavy
    skillet. Add the chicken portions and cook over
    medium–high heat, turning frequently, for 10 minutes,
    until golden brown all over. Using a slotted spoon,
    transfer the chicken to the slow cooker.

3 Add the shallots and garlic to the skillet, lower the
    heat, and cook, stirring occasionally, for 5 minutes, until
    softened. Sprinkle in the reserved seasoned flour and
    cook, stirring constantly, for 2 minutes. Remove from
    the heat and gradually stir in the stock and sherry,
    bring to a boil, stirring constantly. Pour the mixture
    over the chicken and add the thyme sprigs, tomatoes,
    and baby corn. Cover and cook on low for 5–6 hours,
    until the chicken is tender and cooked through.

4 Meanwhile, heat the remaining oil in a skillet, add
    the bread cubes, and cook, stirring frequently, for
    4–5 minutes, until golden all over. Remove and discard
    the thyme sprigs from the stew, then serve, garnished
    with the croutons and chopped thyme.

paprika chicken

ingredients

serves 6

4 tbsp sunflower oil

6 chicken portions

2 onions, chopped

2 garlic cloves, finely chopped

1 fresh red chile, seeded and
    finely chopped

6 tomatoes, peeled and chopped

2 tsp sweet paprika

1 bay leaf

1 cup boiling chicken stock

salt and pepper

method

1 Preheat the slow cooker, if necessary, or according
   to the manufacturer's directions.

2 Heat half the oil in a large, heavy skillet. Add the
   chicken portions and cook over medium heat, turning
   occasionally, for about 10 minutes, until golden all over.

3 Transfer the contents of the skillet to the slow cooker
   and add the onions, garlic, chile, and tomatoes.
   Sprinkle in the paprika, add the bay leaf, and pour in
   the stock. Season with salt and pepper. Stir well, cover,
   and cook on low for 6 hours until the chicken is cooked
   through and tender. Remove and discard the bay leaf,
   then serve immediately.

easy chinese chicken

ingredients

serves 4

2 tsp grated fresh ginger
4 garlic cloves, finely chopped
2 star anise
²/₃ cup Chinese rice wine or
    medium dry sherry
2 tbsp dark soy sauce
1 tsp sesame oil
4 skinless chicken thighs
    or drumsticks
shredded scallions, to garnish
boiled rice, to serve

method

1 Preheat the slow cooker, if necessary, or according
  to the manufacturer's directions.

2 Combine the ginger, garlic, star anise, rice wine,
  soy sauce, and sesame oil in a small bowl and stir
  in 5 tablespoons of water. Place the chicken in a pan,
  add the spice mixture, and bring to a boil.

3 Transfer the mixture to the slow cooker, cover, and
  cook on low for 4 hours, or until the chicken is tender
  and cooked through.

4 Remove and discard the star anise. Transfer the chicken
  to warmed plates and serve garnished with shredded
  scallions with boiled rice.

jambalaya-style duckling

ingredients

serves 4

4 duckling breasts, about
    6 oz/175 g each
2 tbsp olive oil
1½ cups diced cured ham
8 oz/225 g chorizo or other spicy
    sausages, skinned and sliced
1 onion, chopped
3 garlic cloves, chopped
3 celery stalks, chopped
1–2 red chiles, seeded and
    chopped
1 green bell pepper,
    seeded and chopped
2½ cups chicken stock
1 tbsp chopped fresh oregano
14 oz/400 g canned chopped
    tomatoes
1–2 tsp hot pepper sauce
fresh parsley sprigs, to garnish
salad greens and boiled rice,
    to serve

method

1 Preheat the slow cooker, if necessary, or according
to the manufacturer's directions.

2 Remove and discard the skin and any visible fat from
the duckling breasts and cut the meat into bite-size
pieces. Heat half the oil in a heavy skillet, add the
duckling, ham, and chorizo, and cook over high heat,
stirring frequently, for 5 minutes, until all the meat is
browned all over. Using a slotted spoon, transfer the
meat to the slow cooker.

3 Add the onion, garlic, celery, and chiles to the skillet,
lower the heat, and cook, stirring occasionally, for
5 minutes, until softened. Add the bell pepper and stir
in the stock, oregano, tomatoes with the can juices,
and hot pepper sauce. Bring to a boil, then pour the
mixture over the meat.

4 Cover the slow cooker and cook on low for 6 hours,
until the meat is tender. Serve garnished with
parsley sprigs and accompanied by salad greens
and boiled rice.

sweet & spicy pork chops

ingredients

serves 4

4 pork chops, trimmed
    of excess fat
2 tbsp corn oil
1 lb/450 g canned pineapple
    cubes in fruit juice
1 red bell pepper, seeded
    and finely chopped
2 fresh jalapeño chiles, seeded
    and finely chopped
1 onion, finely chopped
1 tbsp chopped fresh cilantro
½ cup boiling chicken stock
salt and pepper
fresh cilantro sprigs, to garnish
tortillas, to serve

method

1 Preheat the slow cooker, if necessary, or according
    to the manufacturer's directions.

2 Season the chops with salt and pepper. Heat the oil
    in a large, heavy skillet. Add the chops and cook over
    medium heat for 2–3 minutes each side until lightly
    browned. Transfer them to the slow cooker. Drain the
    pineapple, reserving the juice, and set aside.

3 Add the bell pepper, chiles, and onion to the skillet
    and cook, stirring occasionally, for 5 minutes until the
    onion is softened. Transfer the mixture to the slow
    cooker and add the cilantro and stock, together with
    ½ cup of the reserved pineapple juice. Cover and cook
    on low for 6 hours until the chops are tender.

4 Add the reserved pineapple to the slow cooker,
    re-cover, and cook on high for 15 minutes. Garnish
    with fresh cilantro sprigs and serve immediately,
    with tortillas.

hearty sausage & beans

ingredients

serves 4

2 tbsp sunflower oil
2 onions, chopped
2 garlic cloves, finely chopped
²/₃ cup chopped bacon
1 lb 2 oz/500 g pork sausage links
14 oz/400 g canned navy beans,
   red kidney beans, or
   black-eyed peas, drained
   and rinsed
2 tbsp chopped fresh parsley
²/₃ cup boiling beef stock
4 slices French bread and ¹/₂ cup
   grated Swiss cheese, to serve

method

1 Preheat the slow cooker, if necessary, or according
   to the manufacturer's directions.

2 Heat the oil in a heavy skillet. Add the onions and cook
   over low heat, stirring occasionally, for 5 minutes until
   softened. Add the garlic, bacon, and sausage links, and
   cook, stirring and turning the sausages occasionally, for
   5 minutes more.

3 Using a slotted spoon, transfer the mixture from the
   skillet to the slow cooker. Add the beans, parsley, and
   beef stock, then cover, and cook on low for 6 hours.

4 Preheat the broiler. Just before serving, lightly toast the
   bread. Divide the grated cheese between the toast
   slices and place under the broiler until the cheese has
   just melted.

5 Ladle the stew onto warmed plates, top each portion
   with the cheese-toast, and serve.

jambalaya

ingredients

serves 6

½ tsp cayenne pepper
½ tsp freshly ground black pepper
1 tsp salt
2 tsp chopped fresh thyme
12 oz/350 g skinless, boneless
    chicken breasts, diced
2 tbsp corn oil
2 onions, chopped
2 garlic cloves, finely chopped
2 green bell peppers,
    seeded and chopped
2 celery stalks, chopped
⅔ cup chopped smoked ham
generous 1 cup sliced
    chorizo sausage, skinned
    and sliced
14 oz/400 g canned chopped
    tomatoes
2 tbsp tomato paste
1 cup chicken stock
1 lb/450 g peeled raw shrimp
2⅓ cups cooked rice
snipped fresh chives, to garnish

method

1 Preheat the slow cooker, if necessary, or according
  to the manufacturer's directions.

2 Combine the cayenne, black pepper, salt, and thyme
  in a bowl. Add the chicken and toss to coat. Heat the
  oil in a large, heavy pan. Add the onions, garlic, bell
  peppers, and celery and cook over low heat, stirring
  occasionally, for 5 minutes. Add the chicken and cook
  over medium heat, stirring frequently, for 5 minutes
  more until golden all over. Stir in the ham, chorizo,
  tomatoes, tomato paste, and stock and bring to a boil.

3 Transfer the mixture to the slow cooker. Cover and
  cook on low for 6 hours. Add the shrimp and rice,
  re-cover, and cook on high for 30 minutes.

4 Taste and adjust the seasoning, if necessary. Transfer
  to warmed plates, garnish with chives, and serve the
  jambalaya immediately.

asian pork

ingredients

serves 4

1 lb/450 g lean boneless pork
1½ tbsp all-purpose flour
1–2 tbsp peanut oil
1 onion, cut into small wedges
2–3 garlic cloves, chopped
1-inch/2.5 cm piece fresh ginger, grated
1 red bell pepper, seeded and sliced
1 green bell pepper, seeded and sliced
1 tbsp tomato paste
1¼ cups chicken stock
8 oz/225 g canned pineapple chunks in natural juice
1–1½ tbsp dark soy sauce
1½ tbsp rice vinegar
4 scallions, diagonally sliced, to garnish

method

1 Preheat the slow cooker, if necessary, or according to the manufacturer's directions.

2 Trim off all visible fat from the pork and cut the meat into 1-inch/2.5 cm chunks. Spread out the flour in a shallow dish, add the pork, and toss well to coat, shaking off any excess. Reserve the remaining flour.

3 Heat the oil in a heavy skillet. Add the onion, garlic, ginger, and bell peppers and cook over low heat, stirring occasionally, for 5 minutes, until softened. Add the pork, increase the heat, and cook, stirring frequently, for 5 minutes, until browned all over. Sprinkle in the reserved flour and cook, stirring constantly, for 2 minutes, then remove the skillet from the heat.

4 Combine the tomato paste with the stock in a pitcher, then gradually stir into the skillet. Drain the pineapple, reserving the juice. Stir the juice and soy sauce into the skillet. Return the skillet to the heat and bring to a boil, stirring constantly. Transfer to the slow cooker, cover, and cook on low for 5–6 hours.

5 Stir in the pineapple and vinegar, re-cover, and cook on high for 30 minutes. Serve garnished with the scallions.

italian slow-braised beef

ingredients

serves 6

1¼ cups red wine

4 tbsp olive oil

1 celery stalk, chopped

2 shallots, sliced

4 garlic cloves, finely chopped

1 bay leaf

10 fresh basil leaves,
  plus extra to garnish

3 fresh parsley sprigs

pinch of grated nutmeg

pinch of ground cinnamon

2 cloves

3 lb 5 oz/1.5 kg beef pot roast

1–2 garlic cloves, thinly sliced

⅓ cup chopped bacon or pancetta

14 oz/400 g canned chopped
  tomatoes

2 tbsp tomato paste

salt and pepper

method

1 Preheat the slow cooker, if necessary, or according
to the manufacturer's directions.

2 Combine the wine, 2 tablespoons of the olive oil, the
celery, shallots, garlic, herbs, and spices in a large,
nonmetallic bowl. Add the beef, cover, and marinate,
turning occasionally, for 12 hours.

3 Drain the beef, reserving the marinade, and pat dry
with paper towels. Make small incisions all over the
beef using a sharp knife. Insert a slice of garlic and a
piece of bacon in each "pocket." Heat the remaining
oil in a large skillet. Add the meat and cook over
medium heat, turning frequently, until browned
all over. Transfer the beef to the slow cooker.

4 Strain the reserved marinade into the skillet and bring
to a boil. Stir in the tomatoes and tomato paste. Stir
well, then pour the mixture over the beef. Cover and
cook on low for about 9 hours until tender. If possible,
turn the beef over halfway through the cooking time
and re-cover the slow cooker immediately. To serve,
remove the beef and place on a carving board. Cover
with foil and let stand for 10–15 minutes to firm up.
Cut into slices and transfer to a platter. Spoon the
sauce over it and serve immediately.

beef & pumpkin stew

ingredients

serves 6

1 lb/450 g braising beef
3½ cups diced pumpkin
   or other squash
1 onion, chopped
1 red bell pepper, seeded
   and chopped
2 garlic cloves, finely chopped
1-inch/2.5-cm piece fresh ginger,
   finely chopped
1 tbsp sweet or hot paprika
1 cup beef stock
14 oz/400 g canned chopped
   tomatoes
14 oz/400 g canned chick peas,
   drained and rinsed
14 oz/400 g canned black-eyed
   peas, drained and rinsed
salt and pepper

method

1 Preheat the slow cooker, if necessary, or according to the manufacturer's directions.

2 Trim off any visible fat from the beef, then dice the meat. Heat a large, heavy pan without adding any extra fat. Add the meat and cook, stirring constantly, for a few minutes until browned all over. Stir in the pumpkin, onion, bell pepper, garlic and ginger, and cook for 1 minute, then add the paprika, stock, and tomatoes, and bring to a boil.

3 Transfer the mixture to the slow cooker, cover, and cook on low for 7 hours. Add the chick peas and black-eyed peas to the stew and season to taste with salt and pepper. Re-cover and cook on high for 30 minutes, then serve.

beef bourguinon

ingredients

serves 6

1 cup diced bacon

2 tbsp all-purpose flour

2 lb/900 g braising beef, trimmed and cut into 1-inch/2.5 cm cubes

3 tbsp olive oil

2 tbsp butter

12 pearl onions or shallots

2 garlic cloves, finely chopped

²/₃ cup beef stock

2 cups full-bodied red wine

1 bouquet garni

2 cups sliced mushrooms

salt and pepper

method

1 Preheat the slow cooker, if necessary, or according to the manufacturer's directions.

2 Cook the bacon in a large, heavy pan, stirring occasionally, until the fat runs and the pieces are crisp. Meanwhile, spread out the flour on a plate and season with salt and pepper. Toss the beef cubes in the flour to coat, shaking off any excess. Using a slotted spoon, transfer the bacon to a plate. Add the oil to the pan. When it is hot, add the beef cubes and cook, in batches, stirring occasionally, for 5 minutes until the beef is browned all over. Transfer to the plate with a slotted spoon.

3 Add the butter to the pan. When it has melted, add the onions and garlic and cook, stirring occasionally, for 5 minutes. Return the bacon and beef to the pan and pour in the stock and wine. Bring to a boil.

4 Transfer the mixture to the slow cooker and add the bouquet garni. Cover and cook on low for 7 hours until the meat is tender.

5 Add the mushrooms to the slow cooker and stir well. Re-cover and cook on high for 15 minutes. Remove and discard the bouquet garni. Adjust the seasoning if necessary, then serve immediately.

mediterranean lamb with apricots & pistachio nuts

ingredients

serves 4

1½ tbsp all-purpose flour
1 tsp ground coriander
½ tsp ground cumin
½ tsp ground allspice
1 lb/450 g boneless lamb leg
    steaks, cut into 1-inch/
    2.5 cm chunks
1 tbsp olive oil
1 onion, chopped
2–3 garlic cloves, chopped
2 cups lamb or chicken stock
pinch of saffron threads,
    infused in 2 tbsp water
1 cinnamon stick
scant ½ cup chopped dried
    apricots
1⅓ cups sliced zucchini
4 oz/115 g cherry tomatoes
1 tbsp chopped fresh cilantro
salt and pepper
2 tbsp coarsely chopped
    pistachios, to garnish
couscous or rice, to serve

method

1 Preheat the slow cooker, if necessary, or according to the manufacturer's directions.

2 Combine the flour, coriander, cumin, and allspice in a shallow dish, add the lamb, and toss until well coated. Reserve the remaining spiced flour.

3 Heat the oil in a heavy skillet. Add the onion and garlic and cook over low heat, stirring occasionally, for 5 minutes, until softened. Add the pieces of lamb, increase the heat to high, and cook, stirring frequently, for 3 minutes, until browned on all sides. Sprinkle in the reserved spiced flour and cook, stirring constantly, for 2 minutes, then remove the skillet from the heat.

4 Gradually stir in the stock and the saffron with its soaking liquid. Return the skillet to the heat and bring to a boil, stirring constantly. Transfer the mixture to the slow cooker and add the cinnamon stick, apricots, zucchini, and tomatoes. Cover and cook on low for 8 hours, until the meat is tender.

5 Remove and discard the cinnamon stick. Stir in the cilantro, season to taste with salt and pepper, sprinkle with the pistachios, and serve with couscous or rice.

bouillabaisse

ingredients

serves 6

5 lb/2.25 kg mixed white fish, such as red snapper, porgy, sea bass, monkfish and whiting, filleted and bones and heads reserved, if possible

1 lb/450 g raw shrimp, peeled and deveined, shells and heads reserved, if possible

grated rind of 1 orange

pinch of saffron threads

4 garlic cloves, finely chopped

1 cup olive oil

2 onions, finely chopped

1 leek, thinly sliced

4 potatoes, thinly sliced

2 large tomatoes, peeled and chopped

1 bunch fresh flat-leaf parsley, chopped

1 fresh fennel sprig

1 fresh thyme sprig

1 bay leaf

2 cloves

6 black peppercorns

1 strip orange rind

sea salt

crusty bread or croutons, to serve

method

1 Preheat the slow cooker, if necessary, or according to the manufacturer's directions.

2 Cut the fish fillets into bite-size pieces. Place the chunks of fish and the shrimp in a large bowl. Sprinkle with the grated orange rind, saffron, half the garlic, and 2 tablespoons of the oil. Cover and set aside in the refrigerator.

3 Put the remaining garlic, the onions, leek, potatoes, tomatoes, parsley, fennel, thyme, bay leaf, cloves, peppercorns, and strip of orange rind in the slow cooker. Add the fish heads and bones, if using, and the shrimp shells and heads. Pour in the remaining olive oil and enough boiling water to cover the ingredients by 1 inch. Season with sea salt. Cover and cook on low for 8 hours.

4 Strain the stock and return the liquid to the slow cooker. Discard the flavorings, fish and shrimp trimmings but retain the vegetables and return them to the slow cooker if you like. Add the fish and shrimp mixture, re-cover, and cook on high for 30 minutes until the fish is cooked through and flakes easily with the point of a knife.

5 Ladle into warmed bowls and serve with crusty bread or croutons.

moroccan sea bass

ingredients

serves 2

2 tbsp olive oil
2 onions, chopped
2 garlic cloves, finely chopped
2 carrots, finely chopped
1 fennel bulb, finely chopped
½ tsp ground cumin
½ tsp ground cloves
1 tsp ground coriander
pinch of saffron threads
1¼ cups fish stock
1 preserved or fresh lemon
2 lb/900 g sea bass, cleaned
salt and pepper

method

1 Preheat the slow cooker, if necessary, or according to the manufacturer's directions.

2 Heat the oil in a large, heavy pan. Add the onions, garlic, carrots, and fennel and cook over medium heat, stirring occasionally, for 5 minutes. Stir in all the spices and cook, stirring, for 2 minutes more. Pour in the stock, season with salt and pepper, and bring to a boil.

3 Transfer the mixture to the slow cooker. Cover and cook on low for 6 hours or until the vegetables are tender.

4 Rinse the preserved lemon if using. Discard the fish head if you like. Slice the lemon and place the slices in the fish cavity, then place the fish in the slow cooker. Re-cover and cook on high for 30–45 minutes until the flesh flakes easily with the point of a knife.

5 Carefully transfer the fish to a platter and spoon the vegetables around it. Cover and keep warm. Transfer the cooking liquid to a pan and boil for a few minutes until reduced. Spoon it over the fish and serve.

vegetable curry

ingredients

serves 4-6

2 tbsp vegetable oil

1 tsp cumin seeds

1 onion, sliced

2 curry leaves

1-inch/2.5 cm piece fresh ginger,
    finely chopped

2 fresh red chiles, seeded and
    chopped

2 tbsp curry paste

2 carrots, sliced

1½ cups snow peas

1 head cauliflower, cut into florets

3 tomatoes, peeled and chopped

¾ cup frozen peas, thawed

½ tsp ground turmeric

⅔–1 cup boiling vegetable
    or chicken stock

salt and pepper

method

1 Preheat the slow cooker, if necessary, or according
    to the manufacturer's directions.

2 Heat the oil in a large, heavy pan. Add the cumin seeds
    and cook, stirring constantly, for 1–2 minutes until they
    give off their aroma and begin to pop. Add the onion
    and curry leaves and cook, stirring occasionally, for
    5 minutes until the onion has softened. Add the ginger
    and chiles and cook, stirring occasionally, for 1 minute.

3 Stir in the curry paste and cook, stirring, for 2 minutes,
    then add the carrots, snow peas, and cauliflower
    florets. Cook for 5 minutes, then add the tomatoes,
    peas, and turmeric, and season with salt and pepper.
    Cook for 3 minutes, then add ⅔ cup of the stock, and
    bring to a boil.

4 Transfer the mixture to the slow cooker. If the
    vegetables are not covered, add more hot stock, then
    cover, and cook on low for 5 hours until tender.
    Remove and discard the curry leaves before serving.

variation

For a creamier curry, stir in ½ cup of coconut milk at the
end of cooking and heat through before serving.

vegetable goulash

ingredients

serves 4

¼ cup chopped sun-dried
  tomatoes
2 tbsp olive oil
½–1 tsp crushed dried chiles
2–3 garlic cloves, chopped
1 large onion, cut into small
  wedges
1 small celeriac, cut into
  small chunks
8 oz/225 g carrots, sliced
8 oz/225 g new potatoes,
  cut into chunks
1¼ cups chopped acorn squash
2 tbsp tomato paste
1¼ cups vegetable stock
1 cup green lentils
1–2 tsp hot paprika
3 fresh thyme sprigs,
  plus extra to garnish
1 lb/450 g tomatoes, chopped
sour cream, to serve

method

1 Preheat the slow cooker, if necessary, or according
  to the manufacturer's directions.

2 Put the sun-dried tomatoes in a small heatproof bowl,
  add freshly boiled water to cover, and let soak for
  15–20 minutes.

3 Heat the oil in a heavy pan. Add the chiles, garlic,
  onion, celery root, carrots, potatoes, and squash and
  cook over medium–low heat, stirring frequently, for
  5–8 minutes, until softened. Combine the tomato
  paste with the stock in a pitcher and stir it into the pan.
  Add the lentils, sun-dried tomatoes with their soaking
  liquid, the paprika, and thyme and bring to a boil.

4 Transfer the mixture to the slow cooker, cover, and
  cook on low for 4½ hours. Add the tomatoes, re-cover,
  and cook on high for 45 minutes, until all the
  vegetables and lentils are tender. Remove and discard
  the thyme sprigs. Serve the goulash topped with sour
  cream and garnished with extra thyme sprigs.

moroccan vegetables

ingredients

serves 4

4 tomatoes, peeled, seeded, and chopped
3 cups vegetable stock
1 onion, sliced
2 carrots, diagonally sliced
1 tbsp chopped fresh cilantro
1⅓ cups sliced zucchini
1 small turnip, cubed
15 oz/425 g canned garbanzo beans, drained and rinsed
½ tsp ground turmeric
¼ tsp ground ginger
¼ tsp ground cinnamon
1⅓ cups couscous
salt
fresh cilantro sprigs, to garnish

method

1 Preheat the slow cooker, if necessary, or according to the manufacturer's directions.

2 Put half the tomatoes in a blender or food processor and process until smooth. Scrape into a pan, add 2 cups of the stock, and bring to a boil. Pour the mixture into the slow cooker, add the remaining tomatoes, the onion, carrots, cilantro, zucchini, turnip, garbanzos, turmeric, ginger, and cinnamon, and stir well. Cover and cook on high for 3 hours.

3 Just before serving, bring the remaining stock to a boil in a large pan. Add a pinch of salt and sprinkle in the couscous, stirring constantly. Remove the pan from the heat, cover, and let stand for 5 minutes.

4 Fluff up the grains of couscous with a fork and divide it among 4 plates. Top with the vegetable stew, garnish with cilantro sprigs, and serve.

sweet & sour sicilian pasta

ingredients

serves 4

4 tbsp olive oil
1 large red onion, sliced
2 garlic cloves, finely chopped
2 red bell peppers,
    seeded and sliced
2 zucchini, cut into batons
1 eggplant, cut into batons
2 cups bottled strained tomatoes
4 tbsp lemon juice
2 tbsp balsamic vinegar
½ cup pitted black olives,
    sliced
1 tbsp sugar
14 oz/400 g dried fettucine
    or pappardelle
salt and pepper
fresh flat-leaf parsley sprigs,
    to garnish

method

1 Preheat the slow cooker, if necessary, or according to the manufacturer's directions.

2 Heat the oil in a large, heavy pan. Add the onion, garlic, and bell peppers and cook over low heat, stirring occasionally, for 5 minutes. Add the zucchini and eggplant and cook, stirring occasionally, for 5 minutes more. Stir in the strained tomatoes and ²/₃ cup water and bring to a boil. Stir in the lemon juice, vinegar, olives, and sugar and season with salt and pepper.

3 Transfer the mixture to the slow cooker. Cover and cook on low for 5 hours until all the vegetables are tender.

4 To cook the pasta, bring a large pan of lightly salted water to a boil. Add the fettuccine and bring back to a boil. Cook for 10–12 minutes until the pasta is tender but still firm to the bite. Drain and transfer to a warmed serving dish. Spoon the vegetable mixture over the pasta, toss lightly, garnish with parsley, and serve.

desserts

chocolate mousse

ingredients

serves 6

1¼ cups light cream
1¼ cups milk
8 oz/225 g bittersweet chocolate,
    broken into small pieces
1 extra large egg
4 egg yolks
4 tbsp superfine sugar
²/₃ cup heavy cream
grated chocolate curls,
    to decorate

method

1 Preheat the slow cooker, if necessary, or according to the manufacturer's directions.

2 Pour the light cream and milk into a pan and add the chocolate. Set the pan over very low heat and stir until the chocolate has melted and the mixture is smooth. Remove from the heat and let cool for 10 minutes.

3 Beat together the egg, egg yolks, and sugar in a bowl until combined. Gradually stir in the chocolate mixture until thoroughly blended. Strain into a pitcher.

4 Divide the mixture among 6 individual baking dishes and cover with foil. Stand the dishes on a trivet in the slow cooker and pour in enough boiling water to come about halfway up the sides of the dishes. Cover and cook on low for 3–3½ hours, until just set. Remove the slow cooker pot from the base unit and let cool completely, then remove the dishes and chill in the refrigerator for at least 4 hours.

5 Whip the heavy cream in a bowl until it holds soft peaks. Top each chocolate mousse with cream and decorate with chocolate curls. Serve immediately.

chocolate & walnut sponge cake

ingredients

serves 4

½ cup unsweetened cocoa,
    plus extra for dusting
2 tbsp milk
1 cup self-rising flour
pinch of salt
½ cup softened unsalted butter,
    plus extra for greasing
generous ½ cup superfine sugar
2 eggs, lightly beaten
½ cup chopped walnuts
whipped cream, to serve

method

1 Preheat the slow cooker, if necessary, or according to the manufacturer's directions.

2 Grease a 5-cup heatproof bowl. Cut out a double circle of wax paper that is 2¾ inches/7 cm wider than the rim of the bowl. Grease one side with butter and make a pleat in the center.

3 Mix the cocoa with the milk to a paste in a small bowl. Sift the flour and salt into a separate small bowl.

4 Beat together the butter and sugar in a large bowl until pale and fluffy. Gradually beat in the eggs, a little at a time, then gently fold in the sifted flour, followed by the cocoa mixture and the walnuts.

5 Spoon the mixture into the prepared bowl. Cover the bowl with the wax paper circle, buttered-side down, and tie in place with kitchen string. Stand the bowl on a trivet in the slow cooker and pour in enough boiling water to come about halfway up the side of the bowl. Cover and cook on high for 3–3½ hours.

6 Carefully remove the bowl from the slow cooker and discard the wax paper. Run a knife around the inside of the bowl, then turn out onto a warmed serving dish. Serve immediately with whipped cream, dusted with cocoa.

lemon sponge cake

ingredients

serves 4

¾ cup superfine sugar
3 eggs, separated
1¼ cups milk
3 tbsp self-rising flour, sifted
⅔ cup freshly squeezed
    lemon juice
confectioners' sugar, for dusting

method

1 Preheat the slow cooker, if necessary, or according to the manufacturer's directions.

2 Beat the sugar with the egg yolks in a bowl, using an electric mixer. Gradually beat in the milk, followed by the flour and the lemon juice.

3 Whisk the egg whites in a separate, grease-free bowl until stiff. Fold half the whites into the yolk mixture using a rubber or plastic spatula in a figure-eight movement, then fold in the remainder. Try not to knock out the air.

4 Pour the mixture into an ovenproof dish, cover with foil, and place in the slow cooker. Add sufficient boiling water to come about one-third of the way up the side of the dish. Cover and cook on high for 2½ hours until the mixture has set and the lemon sauce and sponge have separated.

5 Lift the dish out of the cooker and discard the foil. Lightly sift a little confectioners' sugar over the top and serve.

italian bread pudding

ingredients

serves 6

butter, for greasing
6 slices panettone
3 tbsp Marsala wine
1¼ cups milk
1¼ cups light cream
½ cup superfine sugar
grated rind of ½ lemon
pinch of ground cinnamon
3 extra large eggs, lightly beaten
heavy cream, to serve

method

1 Preheat the slow cooker, if necessary, or according to the manufacturer's directions.

2 Grease a heatproof bowl and set aside. Place the panettone on a deep plate and sprinkle with the Marsala wine.

3 Pour the milk and cream into a pan and add the sugar, lemon rind, and cinnamon. Gradually bring to a boil over low heat, stirring until the sugar has dissolved. Remove the pan from the heat and let cool slightly, then pour the mixture onto the beaten eggs, beating constantly.

4 Place the panettone in the prepared bowl, pour in the egg mixture and cover with foil. Place in the slow cooker and add enough boiling water to come about one-third of the way up the side of the bowl. Cover and cook on high for 2½ hours until set.

5 Remove the bowl from the slow cooker and discard the foil. Let cool, then chill in the refrigerator until required. Loosen the sides of the pudding with a knife and turn out onto a serving dish. Serve with cream on the side.

rice pudding

ingredients

serves 4

²/₃ cup short-grain rice
4 cups milk
generous ¹/₂ cup sugar
1 tsp vanilla extract
ground cinnamon and 4 cinnamon
    sticks, to decorate

method

1 Preheat the slow cooker, if necessary, or according to the manufacturer's directions.

2 Rinse the rice well under cold running water and drain thoroughly. Pour the milk in a large, heavy pan, add the sugar, and bring to a boil, stirring constantly. Sprinkle in the rice, stir well, and simmer gently for 10–15 minutes. Transfer the mixture to an ovenproof dish and cover with foil.

3 Place the dish in the slow cooker and add boiling water to come about one-third of the way up the side. Cover and cook on high for 2 hours.

4 Remove the dish from the slow cooker and discard the foil. Stir the vanilla extract into the rice, then spoon it into heatproof glasses or bowls. Dust lightly with ground cinnamon and decorate with cinnamon sticks.

variation

For a fruity rice pudding, add 2 tablespoons of candied ginger and 2 tablespoons of chopped plumped dried apricots and stir into the pudding before cooking.

thai black rice pudding

ingredients

serves 4

scant 1 cup black glutinous rice
2 tbsp light brown sugar
2 cups canned coconut milk
1 cup water
3 eggs
2 tbsp superfine sugar

method

1 Preheat the slow cooker, if necessary, or according to the manufacturer's directions.

2 Combine the rice, brown sugar, and half the coconut milk in a pan, then stir in the water. Bring to a boil, then reduce the heat and simmer, stirring occasionally, for 15 minutes, until almost all the liquid has been absorbed. Transfer the mixture to individual ovenproof dishes or one large dish.

3 Lightly beat the eggs with the remaining coconut milk and the superfine sugar. Strain the coconut mixture over the rice.

4 Cover the dishes with aluminum foil. Stand the dishes on a trivet in the slow cooker and pour in enough boiling water to come about one-third of the way up the side of the dishes. Cover and cook on high for 2–2½ hours, until set. Carefully remove the dishes from the slow cooker and discard the foil. Serve hot or cold.

apple crumble

ingredients

serves 4

½ cup all-purpose flour

½ cup rolled oats

⅔ cup brown sugar

½ tsp grated nutmeg

½ tsp ground cinnamon

1 cup butter, softened

4 cooking apples, peeled, cored, and sliced

4–5 tbsp apple juice

light cream or yogurt, to serve

method

1 Preheat the slow cooker, if necessary, or according to the manufacturer's directions.

2 Sift the flour into a bowl and stir in the oats, sugar, nutmeg, and cinnamon. Add the butter and mix in with a pastry blender or the prongs of a fork.

3 Place the apple slices in the base of the slow cooker and add the apple juice. Sprinkle the flour mixture evenly over them.

4 Cover and cook on low for 5½ hours. Serve hot, warm, or cold with single cream or natural yogurt.

ginger pears

ingredients

serves 6

6 small ripe pears
1 cup ruby port
1 cup superfine sugar
1 tsp finely chopped candied
    ginger
2 tbsp lemon juice
whipped cream or strained plain
    yogurt, to serve

method

1 Preheat the slow cooker, if necessary, or according to the manufacturer's directions.

2 Peel the pears, cut them in half lengthwise, and scoop out the cores. Place them in the slow cooker.

3 Combine the port, sugar, ginger, and lemon juice in a pitcher and pour the mixture over the pears. Cover and cook on low for 4 hours until the pears are tender.

4 Leave the pears to cool in the slow cooker, then carefully transfer to a bowl, and chill in the refrigerator until required.

5 To serve, partially cut each pear half into about 6 slices lengthwise, leaving the fruit intact at the stalk end. Carefully lift the pear halves onto serving plates and press gently to fan out the slices. Serve with whipped cream or yogurt.

poached peaches in red wine

ingredients

serves 4–6

²/₃ cup water, plus 2 tbsp
²/₃ cup red wine
4 tbsp superfine sugar
1 vanilla bean, split lengthwise
6 peaches, cut into wedges and
    pitted or 12 apricots, halved
    and pitted
2 tsp cornstarch
strained plain yogurt,
    to serve

method

1 Preheat the slow cooker, if necessary, or according to the manufacturer's directions.

2 Pour the ²/₃ cup of water and the red wine into a pan and add the sugar and vanilla bean. Set the pan over low heat and stir until the sugar has dissolved, then bring to a boil without stirring. Remove from the heat.

3 Put the peaches into the slow cooker and pour the syrup over them. Cover and cook on high for 1–1½ hours, until the fruit is tender.

4 Using a slotted spoon, gently transfer the peaches to a serving dish. Remove the vanilla bean from the slow cooker and scrape the seeds into the syrup with the point of a knife. Discard the bean. Stir the cornstarch to a paste with the 2 tablespoons of water in a small bowl, then stir into the syrup. Re-cover and cook on high for 15 minutes, stirring occasionally.

5 Spoon the syrup over the fruit and let cool. Serve warm or chill in the refrigerator for 2 hours before serving with yogurt.

crème brûlée

ingredients

serves 6

1 vanilla bean
4 cups heavy cream
6 egg yolks
½ cup superfine sugar
scant ½ cup light brown sugar

method

1 Preheat the slow cooker, if necessary, or according to the manufacturer's directions.

2 Using a sharp knife, split the vanilla bean in half lengthwise, scrape the seeds into a pan, and add the bean. Pour in the cream and bring just to a boil, stirring constantly. Remove from the heat, cover, and let steep for 20 minutes.

3 Whisk together the egg yolks and superfine sugar in a bowl until thoroughly mixed. Remove the vanilla bean from the pan, then whisk the cream into the egg yolk mixture. Strain the mixture into a large pitcher.

4 Divide the mixture among 6 individual baking dishes and cover with aluminum foil. Stand the dishes on a trivet in the slow cooker and pour in enough boiling water to come about halfway up the sides of the dishes. Cover and cook on low for 3–3½ hours, until just set. Remove the slow cooker pot from the base unit and let cool completely, then remove the dishes and chill in the refrigerator for at least 4 hours.

5 Preheat the broiler. Sprinkle the brown sugar evenly over the surface of each dessert, then cook under the broiler for 30–60 seconds, until the sugar has melted and caramelized. Return the dishes to the refrigerator and chill for an additional hour before serving.

almond charlotte russe

ingredients

serves 4

unsalted butter, for greasing
10–12 ladyfingers
1¼ cups milk
2 eggs
2 tbsp superfine sugar
½ cup chopped blanched almonds
4–5 drops of almond extract

sherry sauce

1 tbsp superfine sugar
3 egg yolks
⅔ cup sweet sherry

method

1 Preheat the slow cooker, if necessary, or according to the manufacturer's directions.

2 Grease a 2½-cup heatproof bowl. Line the bowl with the ladyfingers, cutting them to fit and placing them cut-sides down and sugar-coated sides outward. Cover the bottom of the bowl with some of the trimmings.

3 Pour the milk into a pan and bring just to a boil, then remove from the heat. Beat together the eggs and sugar in a heatproof bowl until combined, then stir in the milk. Stir in the almonds and almond extract.

4 Carefully pour the mixture into the prepared bowl, and cover the bowl with aluminum foil. Stand the bowl on a trivet in the slow cooker and pour in enough boiling water to come about halfway up the side of the dish. Cover and cook on high for 3–3½ hours, until set.

5 To make the sherry sauce. Put the sugar, egg yolks, and sherry into a heatproof bowl. Set the bowl over a pan of simmering water. Whisk well until the mixture thickens, but do not let it boil. Remove from the heat.

6 Carefully remove the bowl from the slow cooker and discard the foil. Let stand for 2–3 minutes, then turn out onto a warmed serving plate. Pour the sherry sauce around it and serve immediately.

index